Anchorage and the Cook Inlet Basin

Volume 10, Number 2, 1983
ALASKA GEOGRAPHIC®

D1567297

The Alaska Geographic Society

To teach many more to better know and use our natural resources

Chief Editor, Robert A. Henning; Assistant Chief Editor, Barbara Olds; Executive Editor, Penny Rennick; Editorial Assistant, Kathy Doogan; Designer, Sandi Harner; Cartographer, Jon.Hersh

About This Issue: This update of Alaska's dynamic Cook Inlet basin and the state's commercial center, Anchorage, was pulled together by staff members, Penny Rennick and Kathy Doogan of Anchorage, and Janet Klein of Homer. Staff member Sharon Schumacher contributed the colorful illustrated maps of Cook Inlet today and "2035." We are grateful to the Kenai Historical Society and to Morgan Sherwood of the History Department of the University of California for their review of the historical content, and to David Stone of the University of Alaska's Geophysical Institute and Gil Mull of Alaska's Division of Geological and Geophysical Surveys for their review.

We thank the many photographers whose images help capture the essence of Cook Inlet country.

Editor's note: Population figures for this issue are from Alaska Department of Community and Regional Affairs, State Revenue Sharing Program for fiscal year 1982.

ALASKA GEOGRAPHIC®, ISSN 0361-1353, is published quarterly by The Alaska Geographic Society, Anchorage, Alaska 99509-6057. Second-class postage paid in Edmonds, Washington 98020-3588. Printed in U.S.A. Copyright© 1983 by The Alaska Geographic Society. All rights reserved. Registered trademark: Alaska Geographic. ISSN 0361-1353; Key title Alaska Geographic.

THE ALASKA GEOGRAPHIC SOCIETY is a nonprofit organization exploring new frontiers of knowledge across the lands of the polar rim, learning how other men and other countries live in their Norths, putting the geography book back in the classroom, exploring new methods of teaching and learning — sharing in the excitement of discovery in man's wonderful new world north of 51°16′.

MEMBERS OF THE SOCIETY RECEIVE *Alaska Geographic*®, a quality magazine which devotes each quarterly issue to monographic in-depth coverage of a northern geographic region or resource-oriented subject.

MEMBERSHIP DUES in The Alaska Geographic Society are $30 per year; $34 to non-U.S. addresses. (Eighty percent of each year's dues is for a one-year subscription to *Alaska Geographic*®.) Order from The Alaska Geographic Society, Box 4-EEE, Anchorage, Alaska 99509-6057; (907) 274-0521.

The cover — *Alaska's largest city, Anchorage; numerous small hamlets, and wilderness surround Cook Inlet in this stylized map of the Cook Inlet basin by staff member Sharon Schumacher.*

Previous page — *Hooligan fishermen scoop up the tiny smelt in their dip nets during the annual hooligan run up Turnagain Arm.* (John & Margaret Ibbotson)

MATERIAL SOUGHT: The editors of *Alaska Geographic*® seek a wide variety of informative material on the lands north of 51°16′ on geographic subjects — anything to do with resources and their uses (with heavy emphasis on quality color photography) — from Alaska, Northern Canada, Siberia, Japan — all geographic areas that have a relationship to Alaska in a physical or economic sense. We do not want material done in excessive scientific terminology. A query to the editors is suggested. Payments are made for all material upon publication.

CHANGE OF ADDRESS: The post office does not automatically forward *Alaska Geographic*® when you move. To insure continous service, notify us six weeks before moving. Send us your new address and zip code (and moving date), your old address and zip code, and if possible send a mailing label from a copy of *Alaska Geographic*®. Send this information to *Alaska Geographic*® Mailing Offices, 130 Second Avenue South, Edmonds, Washington 98020-3588.

MAILING LISTS: We have begun making our members' names and addresses available to carefully screened publications and companies whose products and activities might be of interest to you. If you would prefer not to receive such mailings, please so advise us, and include your mailing label (or your name and address if label is not available).

Library of Congress cataloging in publication data:
Main entry under title:
Anchorage and the Cook Inlet Basin.
  (Alaska geographic, ISSN 0361-1353 ; v. 10, no. 2)
  "Update of vol. 5, no. 1, Cook Inlet Country."
  1. Anchorage (Alaska)—Description.
2. Anchorage (Alaska)—History. 3. Cook Inlet
Region (Alaska)—Description and travel.
4. Cook Inlet Region (Alaska)—History.
I. Alaska Geographic Society. II. Series.
F901.A266   vol. 10, no. 2   [F914.A5] 979.8′3   83-2643
ISBN 0-88240-172-6

Contents

ALASKA

Cook Inlet Basin

Alaska Range

Aleutian Range

Cook Inlet

ANCHORAGE

KENAI

Kenai
Peninsula

HOMER

Scale

30 miles

30 kilometers

A few years back we brought out an earlier *ALASKA GEOGRAPHIC®* special on Cook Inlet and we referred to this dynamic economic heartland of Alaska as "where the action is."

It still is, and in spades. The buildings are getting taller and the homes are creeping farther up the mountainsides.

It's exciting.

Where it will stop nobody knows. See our prophesy for the year 2035. We're not really serious . . . but at the pace the folks around "The Inlet" are setting these days, anything can happen.

Robert A. Henning

President
The Alaska Geographic Society

There is plenty of room to spread out on the sparsely populated west side. Joe Munger, trapper and fisherman, has this view of Chinitna Bay's flatlands from his fish site on Silver Salmon Creek. (Gil Mull)

5

The Basin

Cook Inlet basin is the population and commercial heart of Alaska.

Towering mountains, topped by North America's highest peak, hold Cook Inlet country in a great horseshoe. To the west, the Aleutian Range extends about 160 miles from a point inland of Cape Douglas northward to overlap with the Alaska Range as it curves across the top of the basin. On the east, the Talkeetna Mountains reach from the Alaska Range southward to the Matanuska River Valley. Across the valley, the Chugach Range extends southwestward along the Gulf of Alaska coast to where the Kenai Mountains form a barrier between the turbulent gulf on the south and the surging tides of Cook Inlet on the north.

Within this 37,000-square-mile basin live two-thirds of the state's approximately 400,000 residents, 60% of them concentrated in the Anchorage bowl surrounding the state's largest community.

Two canoeists paddle through the calm waters of Judd Lake, north of Cook Inlet, with the Tordrillo Mountains as a backdrop. (Shelley Schneider)

Two visitors study the distances from Anchorage to various points around the world. This milepost stands in front of the Log Cabin Visitor Information Center on Fourth Avenue.
(Alice Puster)

Many of the extremes in climate that characterize other areas in Alaska are softened by the mountains which shield the region. The Chugach block much of the precipitation from the Gulf of Alaska; the Alaska and Aleutian ranges protect against the ravages of Siberian and high arctic storms. The inlet itself carries marine water into the heart of the basin, where the water moderates temperatures.

Meteorologists classify Cook Inlet country's climate as transitional, a blend of the coastal maritime climate and the continental climate of the Interior. Precipitation at Anchorage is only 10% to 15% of that of coastal communities just a few short miles away on the gulf side of the Chugach Range. For example, Whittier, on the windward side of the Chugach, receives 175 inches a year. Portage, just 13 miles away but on the opposite side of the mountains, gets 58 inches a year.

In winter, the Alaska Range blocks the severe cold of the Interior. Normally, winter temperatures in Talkeetna, 100 miles north of Anchorage, range from zero to 40°; summer readings stretch from 44° to 68°. A little more than 200 miles southwest of Anchorage, Homer, on Kachemak Bay, enjoys a marine climate typical of Alaska coastal regions. In

Above — *Swimmers and sunbathers flock to picturesque Mirror Lake, just 24 miles north of Anchorage on the Glenn Highway.* (Polly Walter, staff)

Right — *Mushers and teams competing in the World Championship Sled Dog Races, held in conjunction with Fur Rendezvous each February, run a course laid out on the streets of Anchorage. Here, spectators line Fourth Avenue to watch the popular event.* (Third Eye Photography)

Homer's case, however, the Kenai Mountains rimming the Kenai Peninsula's outer shore ward off some of the moisture coming from the Gulf of Alaska. Instead of the usual 60 inches of precipitation per year which falls on the outer coast, Homer receives less than half that amount. Temperatures are milder than those in Anchorage. Summer averages range between 42° and 59°; winter temperatures normally fluctuate between 17° and 42°.

Two fingers of land reach toward each other, one from the west side of Cook Inlet, and the other from the Kenai Peninsula just north of the town of Kenai. Known as The Forelands, these two fingers constrict water passage and break up the inlet's currents. In the shallow upper inlet, bays and coves, especially those where fresh water from incoming rivers dilutes the salt water, can be covered with ice. As the ice flows south into warmer water beyond The Forelands, it melts. Only extremely low temperatures for extended periods create conditions suitable for large sea ice build-up in the southern inlet.

Tremendous tidal currents and widely fluctuating tidal ranges contribute to the lack of ice. Cook Inlet tides have a normal maximum range of 34 feet at Anchorage. Exceptions do occur, however, such as that of January 1974 when the tides varied nearly 39 feet. Farther south, at Homer, 18.1 feet is the average diurnal tidal range.

Rivers carry silt from upstream glaciers and deposit it in the inlet. This siltation threatens to close off 40-mile-long Knik Arm and 48-mile-long Turnagain Arm, at the inlet's northern end, and clogs channels north of The Forelands. In the upper inlet the middle channel averages 150 to 180 feet in

Above — *Overgrown with lush green ferns and mosses, a stairway leads to an abandoned World War II lookout post on Outer Island, one of the Pye Islands off the south coast of the Kenai Peninsula.* (Don Cornelius)

Right above — *Canadian dwarf dogwood, or bunchberry* (Cornus canadensis), *is found in many areas of the Cook Inlet region, particularly in birch and spruce forests, and alpine areas up to subalpine zones.* (Nancy Simmerman, reprinted from *ALASKA GEOGRAPHIC®*)

Right below — *Fireweed* (Epilobium angustifolium) *is abundant in the Cook Inlet region.* (Nancy Simmerman, reprinted from *ALASKA GEOGRAPHIC®*)

Above — *The appearance of pussy willows announces the coming of spring along Turnagain Arm. The snow-capped Kenai Mountains rise across the arm.* (Dennis Stacey)

Below — *A heavy snowfall leaves this Girdwood residence blanketed. The area receives an average of 136 inches of snow annually, making for excellent skiing.* (Nancy Simmerman, reprinted from *ALASKA GEOGRAPHIC®*)

Above — *Guests at Silvertip Lodge on Judd Lake relax before departing on a seven-day guided fishing float trip on the Talachulitna River. The river supports rainbow trout, Dolly Varden, arctic grayling, and five species of salmon.* (Shelley Schneider)

Right — *Surf pounds the beach of Homer Spit, a slender finger of land reaching out into Kachemak Bay.* (Annie McKenzie)

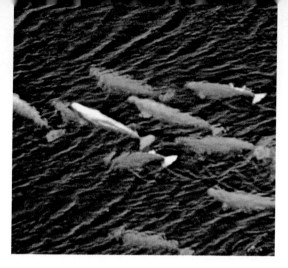

Beluga whales inhabit the inlet each summer, feeding primarily on salmon. (Leslie Nakashima, reprinted from *ALASKA GEOGRAPHIC®*)

Five species of salmon can be found in Cook Inlet. They are, top to bottom: king (chinook); red (sockeye); chum (dog); silver (coho); and pink (humpback). (Nancy Simmerman, reprinted from *ALASKA GEOGRAPHIC®*)

depth. Every year the Corps of Engineers must dredge the silty bottom at the port at Anchorage to keep shipping lanes open. The silt is dumped into a natural channel about 1,000 feet off the dock area, where it is carried away by the currents.

Cloudy water jostled by extreme tides and covered part of the year by ice does little to create a stable environment for marine creatures or salt-water recreation. This does not mean that there is no life in the silty waters, for eulachon (smelt) run up Turnagain Arm, and all five species of salmon follow the inlet to the fresh waters of the Susitna. In fact, great fish runs provided the impetus for the oldest sustained industry on Cook Inlet. Beluga whales and harbor seals follow the fish into the inlet. But by and large, southern Cook Inlet enjoys far more marine recreation and commercial and sport fishing than does the north.

Cook Inlet is actually an extension of the Susitna and Matanuska lowlands, a basin sandwiched among mountains and filled in by layers and layers of sedimentary deposits eroded from surrounding hills.

According to continental drift theory, land masses from far to the south rode northward on shifting plates in the earth's crust. When these land masses bumped into the aboriginal North American continent, some of them slid north by faulting until they reached what is now south-central Alaska.

Seas once covered Cook Inlet country until they were pushed aside by rising mountains eons ago. A chain of

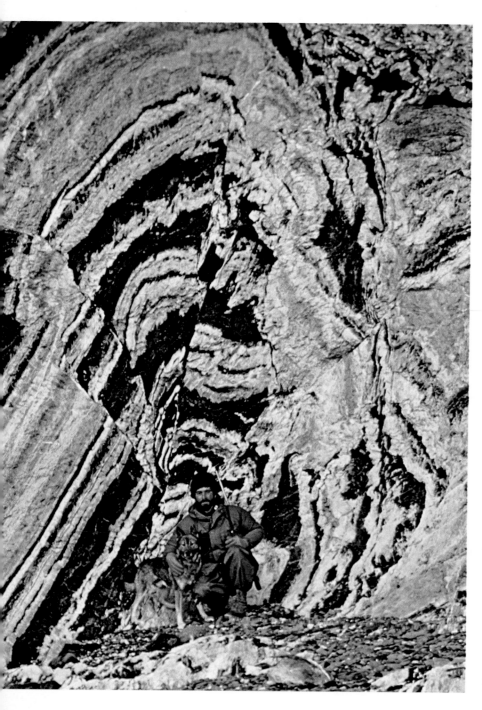

Clockwise from left — *Bruin Bay, across Cook Inlet from the south tip of the Kenai Peninsula, 20 miles west of Augustine Island, is the site of some unusual geologic formations . . . and also the home of quite a few brown bears. Mike McBride, a Kachemak Bay lodge owner, offers some perspective on the size of this coal-laden anticline.* (Mike McBride, reprinted from *ALASKA GEOGRAPHIC®*)

A large crevasse opened down the middle of the Seward Highway just after the 1964 Good Friday earthquake. The quake killed 115 people and caused massive damage to towns and villages in southcentral Alaska. (Art Kennedy, Bureau of Land Management, reprinted from *ALASKA GEOGRAPHIC®*)

A tent is pitched in the shelter of a conglomerate overhang near the McNeil River, on the west side of Cook Inlet. Conglomerate is a mixture of gravel and pebbles, cemented together by finer material. (Steve McCutcheon)

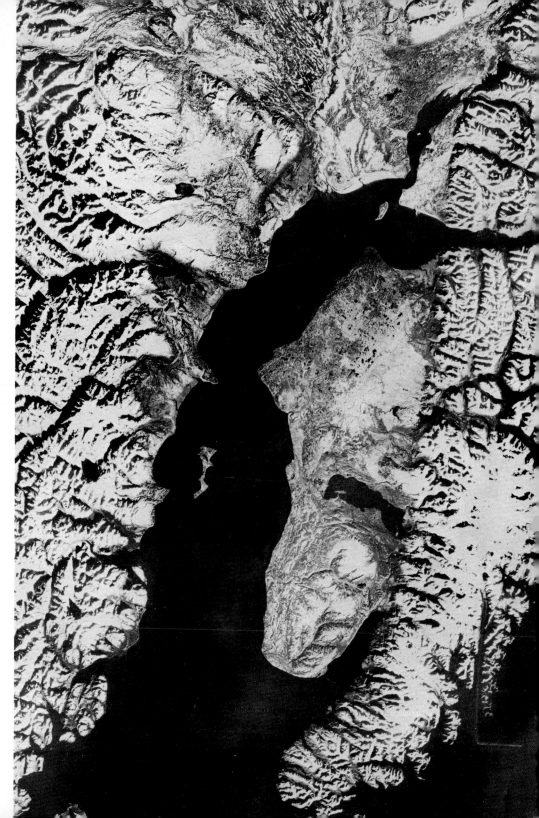

Clockwise from left — *Glassy waters of Cook Inlet reflect two oil platforms. In 1981, oil reserves in Cook Inlet were estimated at 155 million barrels.* (Mel Montalbo)

A kayaker paddles toward Augustine Island in Kamishak Bay, at the southern end of Cook Inlet. Wispy clouds surround the summit of Augustine Volcano, the most active in southcentral Alaska. Augustine last erupted in 1976, blanketing much of the Cook Inlet area with ash. (Don Cornelius)

The Cook Inlet basin is fenced in by dramatic mountain ranges, as this ERTS satellite photo reveals. Cook Inlet cuts through the center of the photo, ending in Knik Arm (top) and Turnagain Arm (reaching the edge of the photo to the right). The Aleutian Range parallels the west coast of Cook Inlet at lower left, blending at upper left with the Alaska Range, which arcs north and east to surround the gulf coast region. Kenai Peninsula and the sharp-edged Kenai Mountains are at lower right in the photograph, penetrated by 30-mile-long Kachemak Bay. (ERTS, reprinted from *ALASKA GEOGRAPHIC®*)

Trimble and Triumverate glaciers rim the jagged peaks of the Tordrillo Mountains, on the south side of the Alaska Range. (Shelley Schneider)

islands rose up in the general vicinity of the Alaska Range, ejecting volcanic debris which settled to the sea floor. Later, uplift and deformation exposed more land from which erosion could carry sediment to the marine basin. This erosion also exposed massive igneous bodies pushed through the earth's crust 250 to 140 million years ago, which now form the core of the Alaska and Aleutian ranges and the Talkeetna Mountains. Erosion from these granitic bodies helped build up the thick sediments of the continental shelf off Cook Inlet. These sediments, mixed with organic material from the ocean's decaying marine life, built the foundation for the Cook Inlet fossil fuel beds.

Mountains surrounding Cook Inlet country range from solitary Augustine Volcano, which rose more than 4,000 feet from the inlet's floor until a 1976 eruption reduced the mountain's height; to mighty Mount McKinley, at 20,320 feet, crown of the Alaska Range and highest peak in North America. Mount Iliamna (10,016 feet) and Mount Redoubt (10,197 feet) sit atop the Aleutian Range on the west. Farther north, where the Aleutian and Alaska ranges intermingle, stand Mount Gerdine (11,258 feet), and steaming Mount Spurr (11,100 feet) which guides pilots through Merrill Pass to western Alaska.

In the Alaska Range, several peaks cluster at the foot of Mount McKinley. From Anchorage more than 130 air miles to the south, Mount Foraker (17,400 feet) and Mount Hunter (14,753 feet) are visible to the west of McKinley. To the southeast of Anchorage, the Chugach, many of whose peaks are topped year-round by glaciers and snowfields, rise 5,000 to 8,000 feet.

Cook Inlet basin was peopled primarily by coastal Eskimos and in more recent times by Athabascan Indians. Although Aleut people were brought to the lower inlet by the Russians to hunt for sea otters and other fur-bearing mammals, their cultural development occurred primarily on the Aleutian Islands.

Geologic Layering

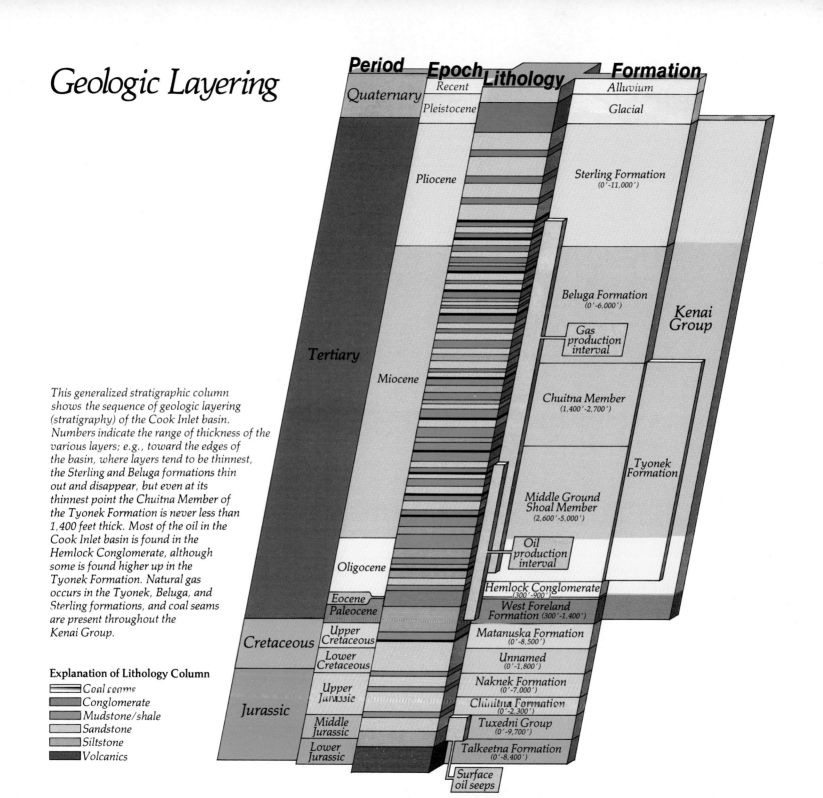

This generalized stratigraphic column shows the sequence of geologic layering (stratigraphy) of the Cook Inlet basin. Numbers indicate the range of thickness of the various layers; e.g., toward the edges of the basin, where layers tend to be thinnest, the Sterling and Beluga formations thin out and disappear, but even at its thinnest point the Chuitna Member of the Tyonek Formation is never less than 1,400 feet thick. Most of the oil in the Cook Inlet basin is found in the Hemlock Conglomerate, although some is found higher up in the Tyonek Formation. Natural gas occurs in the Tyonek, Beluga, and Sterling formations, and coal seams are present throughout the Kenai Group.

Explanation of Lithology Column

- Coal seams
- Conglomerate
- Mudstone/shale
- Sandstone
- Siltstone
- Volcanics

Period | **Epoch** | **Lithology** | **Formation**

Quaternary — Recent — Alluvium

Pleistocene — Glacial

Pliocene — Sterling Formation (0'-11,000')

Tertiary — Miocene

Beluga Formation (0'-6,000')

Gas production interval

Chuitna Member (1,400'-2,700')

Kenai Group

Middle Ground Shoal Member (2,600'-5,000')

Tyonek Formation

Oil production interval

Oligocene

Eocene — Hemlock Conglomerate (300'-900')

Paleocene — West Foreland Formation (300'-1,400')

Cretaceous — Upper Cretaceous — Matanuska Formation (0'-8,500')

Lower Cretaceous — Unnamed (0'-1,800')

Jurassic — Upper Jurassic — Naknek Formation (0'-7,000')

Chinitna Formation (0'-2,300')

Middle Jurassic — Tuxedni Group (0'-9,700')

Lower Jurassic — Talkeetna Formation (0'-8,400')

Surface oil seeps

Eskimos may have been in Cook Inlet as early as the second millennium B.C. They had a stone culture, and evidence of their existence survives in the stone lamps, tools, and household utensils found in middens, or kitchen dumps, located primarily on the islands and shoreline of lower Cook Inlet. Athabascan Indians had a more organic culture with birch and spruce utensils, bone tools, and animal-skin clothing — all organic items that decay rapidly, leaving few artifacts even though Indian occupation of Cook Inlet probably overlapped prehistoric and historic times.

The sea was the center of life for early Cook Inlet peoples. Sea mammals, finfish, and shellfish were food staples. Land mammals provided meat and raw materials for making implements, more so for Indians than Eskimos.

Besides middens and remnants of semisubterranean houses, or *barabaras*, pictographs have been scratched on

Turnagain Pass, 59 miles southeast of Anchorage on the Seward Highway, affords a stunning view of the head of Turnagain Arm. The pass (elevation 988 feet) is a popular recreation area, offering hiking in the summer and skiing, snowshoeing, and snowmobiling in winter. (John & Margaret Ibbotson, reprinted from *ALASKA GEOGRAPHIC*®)

rocks at different points in Cook Inlet country. The pictographs, simple line drawings of men and animals, are thought to be the work of Eskimos. The drawings are found mostly in Kachemak Bay near Bear Cove, Indian Island, and Sadie Cove; but some were found in the 1960s at the head of Tuxedni Bay. All are painted with red hematite, probably mixed with animal fat, and all are remote from known village sites. Like so many other archaeological puzzles, no definite explanation exists for the pictographs.

Left — *The Iditarod Trail was originally blazed in 1910 as a mail route from Knik, on Cook Inlet, to the gold fields of Nome. Strictly a winter trail because much of the ground it covers is swamp and muskeg, the Iditarod is used today for the annual Iditarod Trail Sled Dog Race.* (Staff)

Below — *The aurora borealis arcs over the Tordrillo Mountains. The aurora can be seen frequently on winter nights throughout Alaska.* (Shelley Schneider)

Anchorage: Urban Alaska

It's true what they say — that Anchorage is only a half-hour from Alaska. The wilderness is there. Chugach State Park lies on the city's back doorstep. Moose wander through town. Salmon swim in downtown streams. But Anchorage, more than any other city in Alaska, typifies urban America . . . . Anchorage is urban Alaska.

The 1,955-square-mile Municipality of Anchorage, the area which encompasses the Anchorage bowl, sits on a triangular lowland at the head of Cook Inlet, bounded on the northwest and southwest by Knik and Turnagain arms, and on the east by the majestic Chugach Mountains. The western part of the lowland is a broad plain, sloping gently from the mountains to the inlet, where land and sea are separated by steep bluffs.

The Chugach Mountains, formed of sedimentary and igneous deposits 80 million to 200 million years ago, contain the oldest rocks in the Anchorage area. Millions of years

A summer sunset is reflected in the windows of Anchorage skyscrapers perched on the bluff overlooking Ship Creek. The Alaska Railroad station and yards stretch along the lower foreground. (John & Margaret Ibbotson)

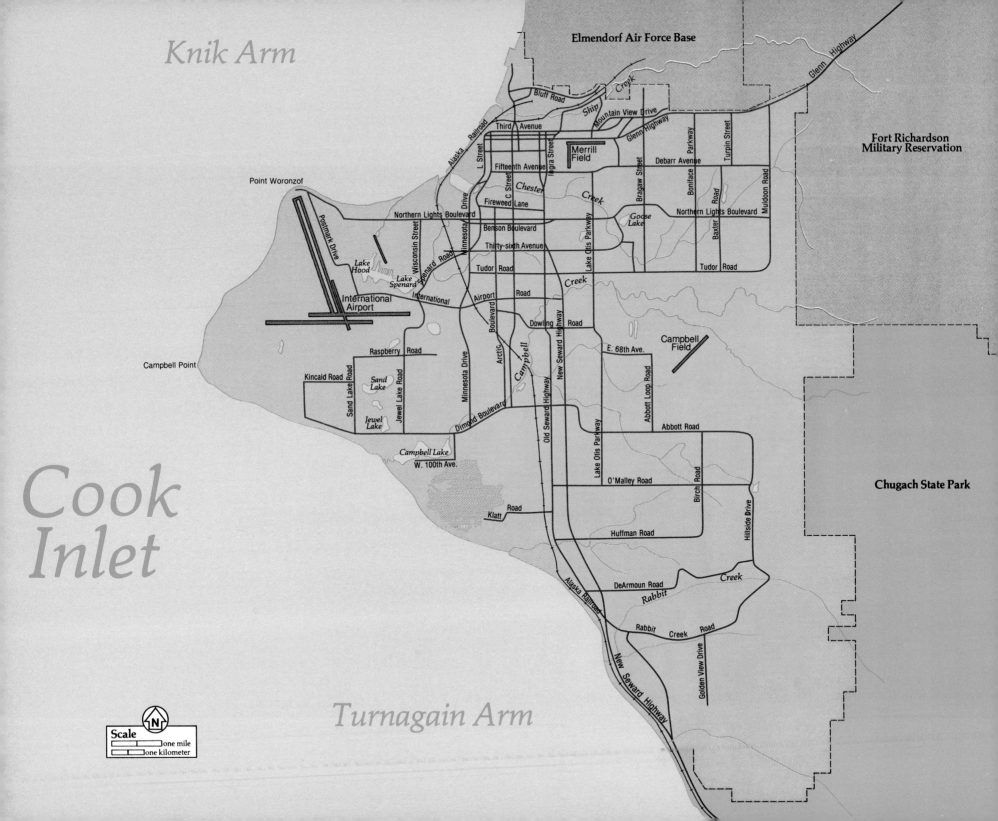

ANCHORAGE

LAND USE MAP

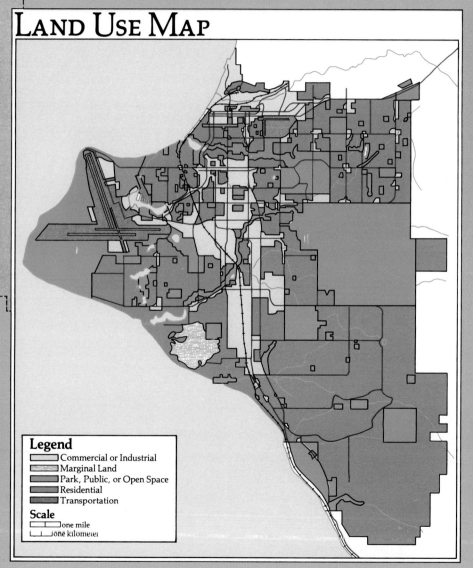

Legend
- Commercial or Industrial
- Marginal Land
- Park, Public, or Open Space
- Residential
- Transportation

Scale
- one mile
- one kilometer

POPULATION BY DISTRICT — 1970-1981

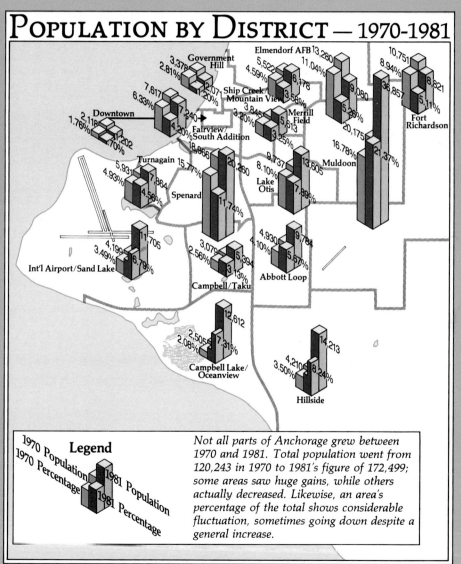

Legend
- 1970 Population
- 1970 Percentage
- 1981 Population
- 1981 Percentage

Not all parts of Anchorage grew between 1970 and 1981. Total population went from 120,243 in 1970 to 1981's figure of 172,499; some areas saw huge gains, while others actually decreased. Likewise, an area's percentage of the total shows considerable fluctuation, sometimes going down despite a general increase.

later, during the Tertiary period, the bowl area's bedrock was laid down when more than 20,000 feet of sand, gravel, and organic material was deposited. The most recent geologic activity took place during the Ice Age, or Pleistocene epoch, about one million years ago. At that time, massive glaciers made several separate advances and retreats, leaving behind a composite of gravel, sand, silt, and clay. Today, an extensive deposit of Bootlegger Cove clay underlies the Anchorage lowland at varying depths, rising nearly to the surface in some areas. Because of its high water content and low stability, this clay sometimes fails under the stress of vibration — as was demonstrated by damage done by the March 27, 1964, earthquake.

Anchorage's geographic setting plays an important role in the city's weather patterns. The city is surrounded on three

sides by mountain ranges, resulting in a mild, semiarid climate, receiving between 13 and 20 inches of precipitation each year, including about 60 to 70 inches of snow (10 inches of snow equal one inch of precipitation).

Most Outsiders are surprised by Anchorage's moderate temperatures, which normally range between 10° and 25° in the winter, with occasional cold snaps causing the mercury to plunge to -20° to -30°. Anchorage in the summertime has been compared with San Francisco: daytime temperatures can reach into the mid-60°s and 70°s, and even though July and August are Anchorage's wettest months, the 14 to 18 hours of daylight allow plenty of chances for a respectable sun tan. The longest day of the year, in mid-June, offers Anchorage 19 hours and 21 minutes of possible sunshine; the shortest day, in mid-December, has only 5 hours and 28 minutes of daylight. Anchorage winters last just about six months: the first measurable snow arrives around October 15 on the average; the latest, around April 14.

Anchorage today is a bustling, growing city; a place where old and new mingle, sometimes in harmony, sometimes in discord. To understand the how and why of modern Anchorage, it is necessary to look back and examine the city's birth and growth.

The stage was set on April 10, 1915, when President Woodrow Wilson selected the route for a proposed railroad connecting an ice-free port with the coal fields of interior Alaska. The route Wilson chose ran north from Seward, using 71 miles of track already laid by the Alaska Central and Alaska Northern railroad companies, west along Turnagain Arm to the mouth of Ship Creek, then north through the Matanuska and Nenana coal fields to Fairbanks.

Several years earlier, politicians in Washington, D.C., had realized that a railroad was necessary if Alaska's rich mineral and resources potential was to be fully developed. In 1914, the Alaska Railroad Act passed Congress and was signed into law, clearing the way for the only railroad in

Above — *Hoarfrost-covered birches reflect the pink of a winter sunset at Russian Jack Springs Park.* (John & Margaret Ibbotson)

Right — *The first snowfall of the year makes recess even more special for Anchorage children. Here, students at Chugach School go for a slide, some using sleds, some just the seats of their pants.* (Polly Walter, staff)

The Chugach Mountains are a stunning sight from just about anywhere in Anchorage. This photo was taken from the midtown offices of The Alaska Geographic Society.
(Penny Rennick, staff)

Following the land auction on July 10, 1915, at which 655 lots on the 350-acre townsite were sold, residents were ordered to move from the tent city. Permanent buildings began going up rapidly, and some of the canvas structures from the Ship Creek flats were moved to new locations on the townsite. This photo shows workers and their horses taking a break while moving the Yukon Rooms, bunkhouse, down Fourth Avenue. (Anchorage Historical & Fine Arts Museum)

history which would be owned and operated by the federal government. Wilson and his secretary of interior, Franklin K. Lane, set up the Alaska Engineering Commission (AEC) to carry out the project, and appointed three men to run the commission: William C. Edes, chairman, a well-known construction and locating engineer; Lt. Frederick J. Mears, an army officer who had been chief engineer on the Panama Railroad construction; and Thomas Riggs, Jr., a mining engineer with extensive experience in Alaska, who would later become governor of the territory.

When Edes, Mears, and Riggs came to Ship Creek in the summer of 1914, surveying possible routes to the Interior, they found only a handful of settlers, all living on the north side of the creek. J.D. "Bud" Whitney, who later worked for the railroad and had a construction camp and station named for him, farmed a homestead near the upper end of Ship Creek. Thomas Jeter lived in a small cabin below the bluff of Government Hill, near the mouth of the creek. A few years earlier, Jeter had been forced to leave a cabin he had lived in since 1909 on Lake Spenard (then called Jeter Lake), as the area was then part of Chugach National Forest and was not

open to homesteading. (Unfortunately, Jeter did not learn from the experience — in 1915, authorities discovered that he had never filed for the land he was living on at Ship Creek. In July of that year he was ordered by Judge Fred M. Brown, federal district judge from Valdez, to vacate the property.)

Two of the first rangers for the recently created Chugach National Forest — Keith McCullough and Jack Brown —also had cabins along the creek. Brown had arrived in 1912 with his new bride, Nellie. He later went to work for the AEC, and the couple moved to a 160-acre homestead and chicken farm in the wilderness near Green Lake, on what is now Elmendorf Air Force Base.

Secretary Lane placed Mears in charge of the Ship Creek headquarters, and he was to direct construction from there northward. (Edes ran the AEC administrative offices in Seward, and Riggs worked from Fairbanks, supervising construction south from that city.) When Mears returned to Ship Creek on April 26, 1915, just two weeks after President Wilson selected the railroad route, he was surprised by what he found. The handful of settlers had grown, spurred by

A Fourth of July baseball game in 1915 drew virtually all of the tent city residents. Officials, concerned about overcrowding and poor sanitation, were making plans to move the entire population to a permanent townsite on the bluff to the south of Ship Creek. (Anchorage Historical & Fine Arts Museum)

rumors of employment opportunities, and Ship Creek had become a booming, ramshackle town of tents, with a population of almost 2,000. Job seekers continued pouring in from all over the Lower 48, and even Europe, at a rate of about 100 per week.

Construction began immediately. The first spike of the Alaska Railroad was driven on April 19, 1915, not by Mears, but by Martha "Babe" White, daughter of the proprietress of the Whitehouse, a canvas-and-frame bunkhouse which served as Anchorage's first hotel.

The tent city was off and running. A post office was opened there in April 1915, with the government adopting the name Anchorage, shortened from Knik Anchorage, another name by which Ship Creek was known. Large boats were able to anchor at the creek, transferring supplies to smaller craft which went on to the settlement of Knik, about 18 miles to the northeast at the head of Knik Arm, which served as a supply center for the Willow Creek mining

Anchorage was first known as Woodrow and Ship Creek. The enduring name, chosen because Ship Creek offered a decent anchorage for incoming vessels, was adopted in 1915. (Courtesy of The Alaska Railroad, reprinted from *ALASKA GEOGRAPHIC*®)

district. On August 9, 1915, residents were allowed to vote on a name for their town. The majority chose Alaska City from a number of suggested names; however, the federal government decided the change was unnecessary, and Anchorage remained Anchorage.

The years 1915 and 1916 marked growth in Anchorage that would be unparalleled until the military boom of World War II. On July 10, 1915, the U.S. General Land Office auctioned off 655 lots on the original townsite. All were sold, at prices ranging from $75 to $1,100. To assure that Anchorage would develop into a respectable community, restrictions were placed on the lots sold: they were not to be used for the sale of liquor, gambling, or immoral purposes; violation of the restrictions meant forfeiture of the property. Andrew Christensen, chief of the Alaska field division of the

land office, presided over the auction. Christensen was Anchorage's unofficial townsite advisor, working closely with the AEC, and served as director of agricultural and industrial development, school system administrator, and all-round troubleshooter until 1920, when Anchorage elected its first mayor.

Permanent buildings began going up immediately after the auction, and by the end of 1915 more than 100 structures had been built, including a much needed school. Installation of water lines, necessary for sanitation and fire protection, began in September 1915, followed closely by telephone service. Electricity, provided by the AEC's steam power plant located along Ship Creek, lit up the town in 1916. Another 1916 improvement was the addition of wide concrete sidewalks along Fourth Avenue, which had been

Andrew Christensen, chief of the Alaska field division of the U.S. General Land Office, presides over the July 10, 1915, auction which sold 655 lots on the new Anchorage townsite.
(Courtesy of The Alaska Railroad, reprinted from *ALASKA GEOGRAPHIC®*)

Above — By October 1915, just three months after the land auction, Anchorage was beginning to take shape as a comfortable small town, with clothing stores, restaurants, and lawyers. (Anchorage Historical & Fine Arts Museum)

Left — In 1915 and early 1916, Anchorage's "theater district" consisted of a small theater in the Byrne's Building on Fourth Avenue between D and E streets. The building also housed an ice cream parlor and library. Next door was the Carrol Building, built in 1915 to house Carrol & Co., men's outfitters. Sydney Laurence, one of Alaska's best known landscape painters, occupied the east half of the Carrol Building for about a year with his photographic gallery and photofinishing business. Note that Laurence's first name is misspelled on the sign; photos taken from different angles show that the name is spelled correctly on the other side of the sign. The Carrol Building still stands on its original location on Fourth Avenue, although the facade has been altered. (Anchorage Historical & Fine Arts Museum)

In late summer of 1916, 12-foot-wide concrete sidewalks were completed along Fourth Avenue, giving Anchorage a more civilized appearance and making things easier for pedestrians, particularly during the muddy spring breakup. The large, modern Empress Theater also was completed that summer. (Anchorage Historical & Fine Arts Museum)

designated as the central business area. Anchorage was taking shape as a modern, well planned city.

Fire protection was provided by Joe Spenard, who ran the City Express, a taxi and delivery service. As his was one of the only autos in Anchorage in 1916, he volunteered to let the city hook up its fire fighting equipment to his car. Spenard, one of early Anchorage's more colorful characters, also opened a resort in 1916 on the shore of Lake Spenard (formerly Jeter Lake) complete with roadhouse, beach, and bathhouses. A wagon road led from town to the resort.

During 1916 and 1917 the population skyrocketed, reaching nearly 7,000 at one point, almost 3,000 of whom worked on the railroad. Construction progressed quickly until mid-1917, when United States involvement in World War I caused a jump in labor costs and created a scarcity of building materials. Because Anchorage's population was based on young, able-bodied railroad workers, 75% of the town's men were subject to the draft in 1917. In early 1918 Mears resigned from the AEC to take command of the 31st Engineer Regiment in France. Many Anchorage men followed his lead and went off to war.

By 1920, construction was completed on the southcentral portion of the railroad, and Anchorage's population dropped to 1,856. The AEC was ready to relinquish its control of the town, but residents had grown accustomed to the efficient government management and were reluctant to take over responsibility for themselves. Finally, following

PHONE 99

TAXI

Christmas Greetings

24 hour
Arts TAXI Arthur Meier
SERVICE

Anchorage got its first "fleet" of 24-hour taxi cabs, made up of two shiny black Buicks, in the mid-1930s. Owner Arthur Meier sent his Christmas greetings along with some advertising for his service. (Anchorage Historical & Fine Arts Museum)

lengthy negotiations and promises by the government to turn over schools, utilities, and streets to the city, Anchorage citizens voted to incorporate. Incorporation became official on November 23, 1920, and six days later Leopold David was elected first mayor of the city of Anchorage. David, an attorney, had come to Alaska in 1904 and lived in Seward, Susitna Station, and Knik before settling in Ship Creek in 1915. Before his election he served as U.S. Commissioner and District Recorder.

In 1923, Ninth Avenue marked the southern boundary of the city, with only wilderness beyond. That spring the entire town turned out to clear a one-block-wide firebreak along the south side of Ninth. The strip of land served as a nine-hole golf course until the late 1930s, and was also used as an airstrip by early-day bush pilots. When Merrill Field was built in 1930 the old airstrip was used only occasionally, such as during spring breakup, when unpaved Merrill Field

was too muddy. Today the strip is officially known as Delaney Park, named for James J. Delaney, Anchorage's mayor from 1929 to 1931; however, it is known locally simply as "the parkstrip."

Throughout the 1920s, Anchorage's population remained below 3,000, and the city evolved into a peaceful, responsible community. The railroad continued to fuel the economy. Mears, who had returned to his position as general manager after the war, resigned in 1923. Several short-term managers followed him; in 1928 the job was taken over by Col. Otto F. Ohlson. Ohlson ran the railroad for the next 17 years.

The ability to live off the land made it possible for many Anchorage residents to get through the years of the Great Depression with a minimum of difficulty. Although unemployment during those years ran as high as 30%, hunting, fishing, and raising large vegetable gardens kept food on the tables. Several New Deal programs helped by providing jobs constructing public buildings and bridges, working on new roads, and making harbor improvements. Raising the gold standard in 1934 gave a boost to the ailing mining industry. At the end of the 1930s came an easing of the economic slump, and Anchorage residents, with the rest of the nation, looked forward to the next decade with high hopes for prosperity.

Prosperity is what they got. World War II and the rapid

The 4th Infantry marches down Fourth Avenue during a 1941 parade, possibly on the Fourth of July. The massive concrete Federal Building, completed just two years earlier, stands in the background. At the time it was built, the structure was the largest and most modern in Anchorage. (Anchorage Historical & Fine Arts Museum)

military build-up, more than any other factors, laid the foundation for the city as it is today. By 1939, the strategic importance of Alaska could no longer be ignored, and Anchorage's central location and accessibility by ship or rail made it a logical place for constructing the bases necessary for defense. Thousands of people and millions of dollars in federal funds poured into the peaceful little town. In 1940

and 1941, two military bases were built in the wilderness on the outskirts of Anchorage: Fort Richardson and Elmendorf Air Force Base. More than 300,000 soldiers came to Alaska during World War II, many of whom stayed or returned after the war to take advantage of veteran's homesteading benefits. In 1940, Anchorage had a civilian population of 4,229; by 1950 that figure had nearly tripled, reaching 11,254.

Anchorage experienced its own construction boom during the war, trying to meet the housing needs of the swelling population. In addition to military personnel and construction workers who did not live on the bases, a substantial number of federal employees from southeastern Alaska were relocated in Anchorage when the government moved

Downtown Anchorage in 1951, here looking west on Fourth Avenue from E Street, appeared sedate and relatively flat. Parking meters, a necessary evil for any growing community, appeared along Fourth in the late 1940s. (M. Peter Vogel)

the headquarters of several agencies here. At least one of those agencies — the Civil Aeronautics Administration — built housing for its employees in the mid-1940s. Much of this CAA construction remains today, as a cooperative apartment complex at Eleventh Avenue and P Street, and a cluster of duplexes along H and I streets between Twelfth and Thirteenth avenues.

The housing shortage in Anchorage became critical during the last years of the 1940s and the beginning of the

In 1958 a neon banner proclaimed Anchorage an All-American City, a title it had won in 1956. Note the two-block section of Fourth Avenue from Smith's Florsheim shoes (just under the hanging stoplight in the center of the photo), at the corner of D Street, to the Denali Theater (right of center). The entire two blocks were destroyed in the 1964 earthquake when they dropped approximately 10 feet below street level.
(Phyllis Mithassel)

1950s. Military families who had been stationed in Anchorage during the war were returning to settle here. In 1947 the government began a railroad rehabilitation program virtually to rebuild the entire system, which brought an additional 280 families to the city.

Anchorage was bursting at the seams: rentals were impossible to find; the crime rate soared; and job seekers, having heard stories of easy employment for big money, were flocking to the already overcrowded town. But despite the problems, the shortage made for a thriving economy. Construction companies were building as fast as they could, and Anchorage was spreading out. By the early 1950s, Spenard had become Anchorage's first suburb, boasting a population of 3,000. In 1951 service began at Anchorage International Airport, and the city was on its way to becoming known as the "Air Crossroads of the World."

Construction booms, the high cost of land and building materials, poor planning, and ineffective zoning requirements are all responsible for the mishmash of architectural styles that adorn Anchorage today. Buildings were thrown up as quickly as possible, with little regard for eye appeal. Old buildings were given new facades according to styles of the period. Businesses crept into residential areas. Some call it quaint, some call it a nightmare, but it's all part of what Anchorage is — gleaming glass skyscrapers next door to log houses next door to Art Deco office buildings.

In July 1957 Richfield Oil Company struck oil in the Swanson River field on the Kenai Peninsula. Exploration was extended to Cook Inlet and met with similar success. Oil companies began opening offices in Anchorage, and the city had finally found a stable base for its economy.

Then, on March 27, 1964, a devastating earthquake measuring 9.2 M_W shook Anchorage for an interminable five minutes, resulting in nine deaths and millions of dollars in property damage. [**Editor's note:** *This magnitude reflects a recent recalculation which resulted in a higher value. The method used (M_w, or moment magnitude) is believed to be a more accurate expression of energy released by strong earthquakes than previously used means of measurement.*] Parts of downtown were a shambles; several blocks along the north side of Fourth Avenue dropped 8 to 10 feet below

Left — Downtown, this section of Fourth Avenue dropped approximately 10 feet below the pre-earthquake street level. (Gil Mull, reprinted from ALASKA GEOGRAPHIC®)

Below — The home of Lowell Thomas, Jr., lays in ruins after the 1964 earthquake destroyed the Turnagain residential area. (Gil Mull, reprinted from ALASKA GEOGRAPHIC®)

street level, destroying historic buildings and the businesses they housed. A section of Turnagain-by-the-Sea, an exclusive residential area on the bluff overlooking Knik Arm, lay in ruins. Disaster assistance arrived almost immediately in the form of rescue units, medical personnel, and federal disaster relief funds. Reconstruction, restoration, and repair began, and parts of Anchorage took on a new and modern appearance.

Anchorage continued to grow throughout the late 1960s and early 1970s, establishing itself as the hub of Alaska commerce and transportation. Construction of the trans-Alaska oil pipeline in the middle of the decade gave one final boost to the city. Although the line does not run near Anchorage, oil companies set up their headquarters here; some of the companies have constructed large office buildings, attesting to the fact that they are here to stay.

In 1975, the city of Anchorage and the Greater Anchorage Area Borough joined forces, creating the Municipality of Anchorage. The municipality is governed by a mayor, an eleven-member elected municipal assembly, and a city manager appointed by the mayor.

Left — *In 1915 city planners designated Fourth Avenue as the central business district in Anchorage. Today, although businesses and shopping centers are scattered throughout the city, Fourth Avenue remains the backbone of the downtown area.* (Bruce Katz)

Below — *Old and new often come together in pleasing combinations in downtown Anchorage. This line-up includes, from front to back: the John Wirum house, built in 1932, now law offices; a modern, mirrored office building; and the newest tower of the Captain Cook Hotel, completed in the late 1970s.* (John & Margaret Ibbotson)

Above — *Judy Gumm of Ester admires the dining room of the recently restored Oscar Anderson House. The house was built in 1915 and is believed to be the first residence completed after the townsite auction. The house has been refurbished with authentic furnishings, and is open to visitors five days a week.* (Penny Rennick, staff)

Below — *The old City Hall has been a landmark on Fourth Avenue since its construction in 1936. It held the mayor's office, City Council chambers, and other local government offices until late 1979, when the municipality moved its headquarters to the Hill Building. Today the structure has been restored to its original appearance and is occupied by a bank and other offices. The interior has been completely refurbished in 1930s style.* (Staff)

Although Anchorage today is a modern city by any standards, much of the past remains. In the downtown area, on the original townsite, the well-preserved homes of Andrew Christensen, Leopold David, and William Edes still stand. Several AEC cottages built in 1916 and 1917 remain along Third Avenue. The Oscar Anderson house, one of the first in Anchorage, has been moved to a new location and restored inside and out, using authentic furnishings of the period. Several larger buildings from the early days — the Wendler, Kimball, and Lathrop buildings are just a few —still house businesses.

As development of the original townsite increases, Anchorage residents are becoming more and more aware of the importance of preserving their past. Old buildings,

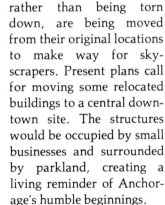

rather than being torn down, are being moved from their original locations to make way for sky-scrapers. Present plans call for moving some relocated buildings to a central down-town site. The structures would be occupied by small businesses and surrounded by parkland, creating a living reminder of Anchor-age's humble beginnings.

Throughout the years, Anchorage has continued to grow with expanded shipping, transportation, communications, and commerce. During the boom brought on by construction of the pipeline in the 1970s, Anchorage was the third fastest growing metropolitan area in the country. By July 1982 the city's population had reached 204,216.

As a shipping hub, Anchorage has several major facilities for handling freight and passengers. Among these is the Port of Anchorage, which has grown from a U.S. Army coal port to the state's largest port facility, handling 1,655,711 tons of freight in 1981. Prior to 1964, roughly 30% of all cargo going through southcentral Alaska ports went through the port at Anchorage; another 60% was handled by the ports at Seward and Valdez. When the Good Friday earthquake of 1964 completely destroyed the latter two ports, freight was

Left — *The Second Avenue home of Leopold David, first mayor of the city of Anchorage, has been well maintained, with very few alterations to the original architecture. The house is presently used as offices by the law firm of Smith & Gruening.* (Polly Walter, staff)

Above — *Old and new frequently rub shoulders in Anchorage. The Wendler Building, which has stood at the corner of Fourth Avenue and I Street since 1915, now cringes in the shadow of the Captain Cook Hotel. Through the years, the structure has served as a grocery store, apartment building, women's club, and restaurant. It remained in the Wendler family until 1982, when Myrtle Wendler Stalnaker sold the building to Hickel Investment Company, owner of the Captain Cook.* (John & Margaret Ibbotson)

Right — *This gleaming mirrored building is headquarters of Cook Inlet Region, Inc. (CIRI), one of 13 regional native corporations set up under the Alaska Native Claims Settlement Act in 1971 to manage cash awards and land selections provided for in the act. Because of a lack of available open land in the area surrounding Cook Inlet, CIRI is the only native corporation allowed to make selections outside its own region. One of the corporation's recent additions to Anchorage's economy was the sale of property in Muldoon to Cook Inlet Housing Authority for the construction of a 120-unit housing project for senior citizens. The project will bear the name of Robert Rude, senior vice president of CIRI.* (Staff)

diverted to Anchorage. Seward's port was rebuilt, but that city never regained the volume of shipping traffic it had enjoyed before the earthquake, and Anchorage became the state's largest port.

A 1982 report outlined $22 million worth of improvements necessary if the Port of Anchorage is to keep pace with the estimated 215% increase in cargo handled during the next 20 years. Immediate needs include 5 to 10 acres of container storage space, and 40 additional acres of land to accommodate future expansion.

Another major transportation center lies in west Anchorage where Anchorage International Airport and Lake Hood floatplane base are neighbors. About 3,720,000 passengers and nearly 20 million pounds of freight went through Anchorage International in 1981. In June 1982 airport officials opened a new international terminal to accommodate increased traffic. About 37 major airlines and smaller air taxi operators regularly use the airport facilities.

Lake Hood, busiest floatplane base in the world with 73,445 takeoffs or landings in 1981, was for many years the only floatplane base with its own tower. Today, traffic coming into the lake has an assigned frequency, but the controller is at the international airport across the road.

Lakes Hood and Spenard used to be separate, but about 40 years ago, when plane traffic increased on Hood and pilots began parking their planes on Lake Spenard, a channel was dug connecting the two lakes. In winter, when the lakes freeze, pilots remove their floats and install skis. Besides planes, Lake Spenard has a fine swimming beach, and habitat for migrating waterfowl as they pass over Anchorage.

Another focal point for shipping is the Alaska Railroad terminal in the industrial/port complex just north of the downtown area. The federally operated railroad, with headquarters in Anchorage, has 470 miles of mainline track running from Seward on the Kenai Peninsula to Fairbanks.

Ice floes in Knik Arm are no deterrent to the year-round operations at the Port of Anchorage, largest in the state. Port facilities are becoming cramped with the increasing volume of cargo handled each year; long range plans call for extensive expansion to accommodate the increases. (Third Eye Photography)

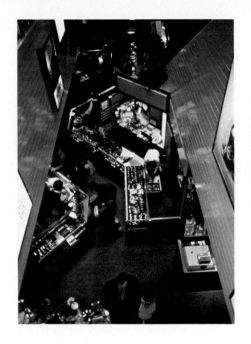

Above — *Passengers browse in the duty free shop, part of the new Anchorage International Terminal at the airport. The $29 million terminal opened July 1, 1982, and is designed to accommodate a peak load of 2,800 passengers. It is estimated that the new facility will serve more than one million passengers each year.* (Polly Walter, staff)

Right — *Major domestic airlines serving Anchorage include Alaska, Northwest Orient, Western, and Wien Air Alaska.* (Nancy Simmerman, reprinted from *ALASKA GEOGRAPHIC®*)

Nine regularly scheduled international air carriers land at Anchorage International Airport. (Nancy Simmerman, reprinted from *ALASKA GEOGRAPHIC®*)

Above — *Merrill Field serves as base for many private airplanes in Anchorage, recording more than 300,000 takeoffs and landings each year. The field was named for pioneer aviator Russell Merrill who lost his life when his plane went down on a flight to Akiak in 1929.* (Polly Walter, staff)

Left — *Colorful floatplanes line the shore of Lake Hood, busiest floatplane base in the world. The lake was probably first used by pilots in the late 1920s; in 1940 a channel connecting Lake Hood with neighboring Lake Spenard was completed. This gave pilots a longer takeoff space, enabling them to carry heavier loads than previously possible.* (Glen Forster)

47

Right — *Two Canada geese rest at Potter Marsh, a favorite bird-watching spot.* (Nancy Simmerman, reprinted from *ALASKA GEOGRAPHIC®*)

Below — *An Alaska Railroad engine prepares to leave the Anchorage yard on its way to Fairbanks, a daily trip during the summer.* (Staff)

A short spur carries passengers and freight from Whittier on Prince William Sound to Portage, 47 miles south of Anchorage on the Seward Highway. During the past couple of years, traffic volume has increased on the railroad. In 1981 the line earned $34 million in freight revenue and hauled 3,362,000 tons of freight. For several years, the federal government has been negotiating to sell the railroad to the state of Alaska, but problems such as price and rights of way so far have prevented the sale from taking place.

Two major highways provide access to and from Anchorage. The Seward Highway takes passengers south 127 miles to Seward on Resurrection Bay on the eastern Kenai Peninsula. About 90 miles south of Anchorage, the Sterling Highway branches off from the Seward to connect communities of the western peninsula to Anchorage. To the north, the Glenn Highway extends 189 miles to Glennallen, where it crosses the Richardson Highway and continues an additional 139 miles to Tok on the Alaska Highway. Thirty-five miles outside of Anchorage the George Parks Highway branches off from the Glenn and follows a route north to Fairbanks and other points in the Interior.

All the goods hauled by trucks, barges, trains, and planes must be stored somewhere, and the place is Anchorage. Incoming freight waits at warehouses for shipment to the Bush and smaller Alaska communities on the road system.

Mom takes a rest after getting her brood settled on a log at Potter Marsh State Game Refuge, along the Seward Highway 10 miles south of downtown Anchorage. The refuge is a resting place for thousands of birds during their spring and fall migrations. (Jon Nickles)

Far left — *This aerial view of Anchorage, taken in fall of 1981, looks west over the city toward Cook Inlet and the Alaska Range. The Glenn Highway, one of two major highways leading to and from Anchorage, heads for the downtown skyscrapers, passing one of the city's many trailer courts.* (Third Eye Photography)

Left — *Northern Lights Boulevard, one of the main east-west routes in Anchorage, is lined with small businesses, fast food restaurants, and every imaginable style of architecture.* (Polly Walter, staff)

Below — *Spenard Road, once a narrow trail cut through the wilderness by Joe Spenard, is now four-lane blacktop, with businesses, bars, offices, and restaurants.* (Polly Walter, staff)

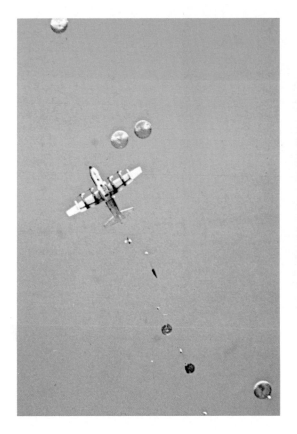

Upper left — *An aircraft based at Elmendorf Air Force Base performs a practice drop.* (U.S. Air Force, reprinted from *ALASKA GEOGRAPHIC®*)

Above — *A crowd takes a look at a C-5A aircraft open for public inspection on Elmendorf Air Force Base. Elmendorf, headquarters of the Alaskan Air Command 21st Tactical Fighter Wing, served nearly 6,500 soldiers and 8,600 dependents in mid-1982.* (John & Margaret Ibbotson)

Left — *This aerial photo shows sprawling Elmendorf Air Force Base, located north of downtown Anchorage.* (U.S. Air Force, reprinted from *ALASKA GEOGRAPHIC®*)

The economy of Anchorage is not as simple now as it was back in the days when the railroad or the military fed the growing community. Today Anchorage boasts a work force of 93,000, with two-thirds of the jobs spread almost equally between government (local, state, and federal), retail trade, and service-related businesses (e.g., auto repair shops, cleaners, barbers). Another one-fifth of the jobs in Anchorage relate to transportation, communications, and utilities, or to the seasonal construction trade.

The oil industry continues to invest in Anchorage. In late 1982, ARCO Alaska, Inc., built a 21-story addition to its downtown headquarters, making it the tallest building in the state. Only two blocks away, the H.L. Hunt family, Texas silver and oil barons, put up a 20-story office tower.

The state's construction industry is not the only one to get a boost from oil. The fuel giants contribute substantially to cultural and civic events, which enhance the city's image as urban Alaska.

Implementation of the Project 80s community development package in 1980 led to construction of a new sports

Vehicles painted with camouflage markings sit in the motor pool at Fort Richardson. The base is home for about 3,500 soldiers and nearly 5,000 dependents. (Polly Walter, staff)

stadium, convention center, performing arts center, expanded museum, and a new headquarters library. Municipal construction, coupled with completion of the new Federal Building, has gone hand in hand with increased private construction. New office buildings, new or expanded shopping centers, and residential development give the city an appearance of vitality and bustle.

Tourism also exerts a considerable influence on the economy, contributing in some way to the employment of more than 7,500 Anchorage residents. In 1981, 785,000 visitors came to Anchorage and left $230 million. The Anchorage Convention and Visitors Bureau operates the Log Cabin Visitor Information Center, located downtown, where travelers can stop by, chat with the staff, and select from a wide assortment of free brochures and maps on places that would be interesting to see and visit.

Clockwise from left — *Paul Norgaard, president of ARCO Alaska, Inc., shows off a model of the company's new 21-story tower in downtown Anchorage. The tower was scheduled for completion in March 1983 and will provide 400,000 square feet of office space. Norgaard has been with ARCO since 1955, and previously served as their North Slope District Manager, in charge of development and operation of the Prudhoe Bay field.* (Polly Walter, staff)

Anchorage's Federal Building and U.S. Courthouse covers three square blocks and is one of the most modern office buildings in the state. The building was completed in 1979 on the $5.6 million site. The structure houses more than 50 federal agencies, plus congressional offices and court facilities. (Polly Walter, staff)

Increasing construction in the Anchorage area created the need for a nearby source of sand and gravel. The need is met by approximately 540 acres of gravel pits located near Sand Lake in southwest Anchorage. Several of the pit operators have been excavating since the early 1950s, when a large amount of sand and gravel was needed for construction of the international airport. (Jim Thiele)

Above — *For any city whose population rises faster than the number of new dwellings, trailer courts offer a quick, if unaesthetic, solution to the problem. Anchorage has its share of courts, such as this one on the east side of town.*
(Polly Walter, staff)

Right — *Utility linemen accompany a late-1930s vintage house on its way to storage at the city landfill. Development pressures in downtown Anchorage have forced relocation of many historic buildings, and preservationists are working to establish a voter-mandated "Railroad Town." The historic village would save the houses by offering them for reuse as professional offices, restaurants, and specialty shops. The house shown here was built about 1938 by Jake Markley.* (Virginia McKinney, staff)

As anyone who has ever visited Anchorage will admit, the city's residents enjoy the best of both worlds: all the amenities of a big city, plus unlimited recreational opportunities just minutes from home.

Chugach State Park, stretching along the eastern edge of Anchorage, is a popular year-round recreation spot. Hiking, berry picking, picnicking, and nature walks are some of the summer activities in the park. Winter offerings include snowmobiling (in designated areas) and cross-country skiing.

Four downhill ski areas are located within the Municipality of Anchorage — Hillside Park, Centennial Park, Arctic Valley, and Russian Jack Springs. All are easy drives from downtown and also can be used by cross-country skiers. Ski trails are maintained by the municipality in several city parks, including the Chester Creek Green Belt, which cuts right through the middle of town.

In 1982, the municipality gained title to a 1,000-acre tract of land at Point Campbell, adjacent to Kincaid Park, for development as a ski area. In mid-March 1983 the seventh race of the eight-race World Cup Nordic skiing championships was held on the Point Campbell property. City officials hope to have the area designated as a possible site for future Winter Olympic games.

Anchorage municipal parks — there are more than 130 of them — are popular year-round. About 100 miles of paved bike trails crisscross the city, doing double duty as ski trails in the winter. Other park facilities include nearly 50 tennis courts, three indoor swimming pools, and several outdoor and one year-round indoor ice skating rinks.

The most important winter event in Anchorage is Fur Rendezvous, which takes place every February. Fur Rondy, as it is called locally, began in 1936 as a fur auction where trappers were encouraged to sell their pelts. The small collection of furs was no competition to the real fur auctions in Seattle, Winnipeg, and New York, but many other activities were added, including arts and crafts exhibits, a carnival, and the Miners and Trappers Ball. Several unusual competitions, such as the beard-growing contest, weight-pulling contest (for dogs only), and the waiter and waitress races, are guaranteed to cure even the most severe cases of cabin fever. A few furs are still auctioned — mostly to local

Dan Alex, president of Eklutna, Inc., explains the benefits of Styrofoam insulation in home construction. Eklutna, Inc., one of many village corporations set up under the Alaska Native Claims Settlement Act to manage land entitlements, is building four homes in Chugiak using the insulation. The corporation has about 150 shareholders, most of whom live in Anchorage. Eklutna is the fourth largest village corporation in Alaska, managing real estate valued at more than $90 million in 1982. (Polly Walter, staff)

Assemblywoman Lidia Selkregg checks her notes during an interview by local reporter Karen Whittaker. Selkregg has represented her east Anchorage district on the Municipal Assembly since 1977. She is also a professor at the University of Alaska, teaching resource economics and planning, and geology and life sciences. Since coming to Alaska in 1958, Selkregg has involved herself with resources, people, and environmental issues. (Polly Walter, staff)

Left — *A skier enjoys the solitude of Chester Creek Ski Trail, which winds through the city. In the summertime the paved trail is used by bicyclists.* (John & Margaret Ibbotson)

Below — *Anchorage Mayor Tony Knowles discusses the Crow Creek Pipe & Drum band with his daughter, Devon, at the dedication of Margaret Eagan Sullivan Park. Knowles was elected in 1981 to succeed George Sullivan, who had served as mayor since 1958. The park was named in honor of Sullivan's wife, a lifelong Alaskan.* (Polly Walter, staff)

carnival spectators, but the event has grown into one of North America's more important winter carnivals.

Winter wouldn't be winter in Anchorage without sled dog racing. Several area clubs sponsor races throughout the season, but the most popular are the World Championship Sled Dog Race (held in conjunction with Fur Rendezvous), and the beginning of the annual Iditarod Trail Sled Dog Race to Nome.

Anchorage's long summer days are filled with a variety of outdoor sports. There are organized softball and soccer teams, which compete for league championships on the

Below — *Jim Hess (left), of Anchorage Auction Company, conducts business amid snowflakes in the Fur Rendezvous' oldest event — the fur auction. Hess, who has been in charge of the auction for the past 22 years, sold more than 4,000 furs during the 1982 Rondy.* (Tom Walker)

Right — *Colorful hot air balloons prepare to ascend into crystal clear February skies for the Fur Rendezvous Hot Air Balloon Race.* (Tom Walker)

Anchorage furrier Perry Green admires a hat and jacket of natural Alaska red fox, modeled by Querida Stepp. Green and his brother, Jerry, are owners of David Green & Sons, Inc., a fur manufacturing firm started in Ketchikan in 1922 by their father, David Green. Today, the Greens operate two factories, one in Anchorage and one in New York, and have stores in Ketchikan, Cordova, Juneau, and Fairbanks, as well as two shops in Anchorage. True to his motto, "if you don't know furs, know your furrier," Green maintains a high profile in the city, and is well known to Anchorage residents as a world class amateur poker player as well as merchant. (Polly Walter, staff)

There's nothing like a rousing game of snowshoe softball to warm you up on a cold winter day. This competition is one of many special events held in conjunction with Fur Rendezvous each February. (John W. Warden)

Patsy James weighs coffee beans in her Fifth Avenue shop, the Kobuk Coffee Company and Gold Pan gift shop. James, who has run the shop for 17 years, was born in Anchorage and presently enjoys having four generations of her family here. The store sells coffee, tea, and accessories, as well as ivory, jade, and other Alaska gifts. The coffeepot is always on, and visitors frequently stop by just to chat, helping James to live up to her objective, "to give our customers a little bit of old Alaska hospitality." (Polly Walter, staff)

parkstrip. Jogging is more than just exercise for the runners who participate in the Mayor's Midnight Sun Marathon or any of the commercially sponsored runs held every year. There is boating on Westchester Lagoon, or, for those who don't mind getting wet, the Campbell Creek Canoe Classic is held each July, featuring boaters, some in costume, riding anything that will float.

If fishing is your bag, but long distance hauls are not, there is plenty of opportunity to try your hand with a rod near Anchorage. Jewel Lake has been stocked with trout, and coho and pink salmon can be caught in Ship Creek. Although king salmon also go up the creek, fishing for them is not legal. Chester Creek sports a remnant population of pink salmon. In summer 1982 Alaska Department of Fish & Game biologists released about 400,000 young coho salmon into Westchester Lagoon near the creek's mouth. Coho fingerlings require two years to reach maturity, and biologists hope several thousand of the fish will return to Chester Creek in the fall of 1984 to be the foundation for a recreational fishery.

Four species of salmon — king, pink, coho, and sockeye — swim in Campbell Creek, but fishing is limited to Dolly

Russian Jack Springs Golf Course cuts through a thick stand of birch trees in northeast Anchorage. The course, which uses artificial turf greens, is open from 7:00 A.M. to 10:00 P.M., June through September. (John & Margaret Ibbotson)

Varden and rainbow trout downriver from Old Seward Highway only. Rabbit Creek, which flows through south Anchorage, has pink salmon, a few kings and cohos, and Dollies. Most of the small streams along the Seward Highway south of Anchorage sustain populations of pink salmon; Bird Creek has the best salmon run between Anchorage and the Twentymile/Portage area.

It's even possible to play golf in Anchorage during the summer. The municipality maintains a nine-hole course at Russian Jack Springs, and two military courses are open to civilians — Moose Run Golf Course on Fort Richardson, and Elmendorf Golf Course.

The Alaska Zoo, about 10 miles southeast of downtown, attracts residents and visitors of all ages. Two of the zoo's most popular inhabitants are Binky, a polar bear, and Annabelle, an elephant.

One of Anchorage's conveniences is the brightly painted double-decker buses called Shopper's Shuttles. The two buses make regular loops between major hotels and downtown shopping areas every day except Sunday. The ride is free. (Penny Rennick, staff)

Above — Urban anglers try their luck at catching pink salmon in Ship Creek, near downtown. (Polly Walter, staff)

Left — The Campbell Creek Canoe Classic, held each June, is a just-for-fun race which always draws a crowd of spectators. Contrary to its name, the race is not limited to canoes. (John & Margaret Ibbotson)

For those with more refined tastes, Anchorage has much to offer in the way of cultural entertainment. Theatergoers can take their pick of performances offered by the Alaska Repertory Theatre, Anchorage Community Theater, Theater Guild, or any of the other local theater groups. The Anchorage Symphony and Civic Opera provide classical entertainment throughout the year, and dance enthusiasts can watch programs put on by the Alaska Contemporary Dance Company or the Anchorage Civic Ballet.

Connoisseurs of the fine arts can also find many diversions in Anchorage. The city boasts more than 20 art galleries, and thousands come to buy or just browse at any of the arts and crafts fairs held around town every year. The Visual Arts Center of Alaska provides studio and public exhibition space for artists from throughout the state and offers workshops for budding artists.

The Anchorage Historical & Fine Arts Museum displays permanent collections of Alaskan artifacts, plus regular exhibits of regional, national, and international art. The museum also sponsors the annual All Alaska Juried Art Show.

Back in 1915, the founders of Anchorage realized that one of their priorities was establishing a decent school system for their children. Today, the Anchorage School District oversees the education of nearly 38,000 youngsters who attend the city's 61 public elementary and secondary schools. Another 2,000 children attend any of several private schools in the area. Post-secondary students can choose between the University of Alaska, Anchorage; Alaska Pacific University; or Anchorage Community College. Combined enrollment for the three schools tops 13,000. Anchorage Community Schools, part of the Municipal Parks and Recreation Department, offer adults a variety of evening classes in the city's public schools. The atmosphere is informal, and subjects offered might include macrame, aerobic dancing, or conversational Japanese.

Left — *Paul Brown has been producing director for the Alaska Repertory Theatre since its premier season in 1977, responsible for overall management of the company. The Rep presents three or four productions each year. Brown, a transplanted New Yorker, has lived in Alaska for 13 years. He has been a strong supporter of the arts in Anchorage, and is currently involved in an effort to increase national awareness of the Rep.* (Polly Walter, staff)

Above — *The Alaska Repertory Theatre, shown here during a performance of Dickens's* A Christmas Carol, *entertains Anchorage with four plays each season.* (Third Eye Photography)

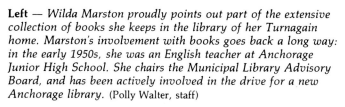

Left — *Wilda Marston proudly points out part of the extensive collection of books she keeps in the library of her Turnagain home. Marston's involvement with books goes back a long way: in the early 1950s, she was an English teacher at Anchorage Junior High School. She chairs the Municipal Library Advisory Board, and has been actively involved in the drive for a new Anchorage library.* (Polly Walter, staff)

Above — *Lanie Fleischer positions a mat for cutting in Perimeters, the custom frame shop she operates in her home. The shop is currently working on putting mats and frames on the private collection of Anchorage artist Byron Birdsall. Since arriving in Anchorage in 1971, Fleischer has been active in community affairs. She was instrumental in the development of the city's system of bike trails, and remains involved with historic preservation.* (Polly Walter, staff)

Above — *Van Hale (left) and Jack Amon pose while making final preparations for a wine-tasting party at the Marx Brothers Cafe, which they own with partner Ken Brown. The cafe is a small, first-class restaurant which opened in October 1979. It is located on Third Avenue in one of the old Alaska Engineering Commission cottages, built in 1916.* (Polly Walter, staff)

Left — *Kay Fanning, editor and publisher of the* Anchorage Daily News, *looks over the latest edition with managing editor Howard Weaver. The morning newspaper is the recipient of several local press awards every year. In 1976, the Daily News won the coveted Pulitzer Prize for a series titled "Empire: The Alaska Teamsters Story."* (Polly Walter, staff)

Above — *Anyone who has the opportunity to watch morning television in Anchorage knows Theda Comstock, hostess of "The Woman's Touch" on KTUU-TV for the last 21 years. Comstock accomplishes her objective, to entertain and educate, by inviting guests from organizations around the city to discuss community issues while they cook.* (Polly Walter, staff)

Below — *Augie Heibert (standing), chairman of Northern Television, Inc., and engineers Cal Lewin (foreground) and Jay Hoppie investigate the capabilities of the company's new Dubner Character Background Generator — a sophisticated piece of video equipment used to create special graphic effects. Heibert started Northern Television in 1953 with KTVA, the first television station in Anchorage. Today, the company has two television stations and several radio stations in Anchorage, Fairbanks, and Valdez.* (Polly Walter, staff)

Above — *Skyrockets explode in a dazzling array of colors during the mid-winter Fur Rendezvous fireworks display.* (John & Margaret Ibbotson)

Right — *Motorists traveling east on Abbott Road, in south Anchorage, have a close-up view of the Chugach Mountains.* (John & Margaret Ibbotson, reprinted from *ALASKA GEOGRAPHIC*®)

The Kenai Peninsula

As diverse as Alaska itself, the Kenai Peninsula is a microcosm of the rest of the state . . . metropolitan areas, small settlements, wilderness, and all levels of development in between. This tour of the Cook Inlet basin begins with the extreme southwestern tip of the peninsula, moves north along the coast of the inlet, then crosses the peninsula's midsection to the mountainous east side. Finally, the tour heads north through the narrow isthmus which connects the peninsula to mainland Alaska.

Flanking Kennedy Entrance where Cook Inlet and Gulf of Alaska waters mingle are the Chugach Islands to the northeast and the Barren Islands to the southwest. Less than 20 miles apart, the two island groups are geologic remnants of the Kenai Mountains, an extension of the Chugach Range which defines lower Kenai Peninsula.

Although Capt. James Cook named them Barren Islands

The rustic community of Seldovia (population 505) depends on fishing, fish processing, logging, and tourism for its economic survival. Isolated from Alaska's main highway system, Seldovia relies on planes and boats to bring in supplies and people. (Helen Rhode)

Above — *This illustration shows Port Graham as seen by Capt. Nathaniel Portlock during his 1786 voyage to Cook Inlet.* (Alaska Historical Library, reprinted from *ALASKA GEOGRAPHIC®*)

Below — *Calm waters reflect this harbor scene at Port Graham, a small fishing community on the south shore of Port Graham, an inlet southwest of Seldovia.* (John Jonas)

because of "their very naked appearance" when observed in May 1778, the islands are anything but barren when seabirds and sea mammals by the thousands return annually to give birth and rear their young. Fifty-five bird species, with an estimated population of 355,000 adult seabirds, feed in the productive waters around the islands, as do sea lions, harbor seals, and whales. The seven named islands, totaling more than 10,000 acres, are part of the Alaska Maritime National Wildlife Refuge under jurisdiction of the U.S. Fish & Wildlife Service.

Northeast of the Chugach Islands, on the mainland, the Kenai Mountains reach the sea at the tip of the Kenai Peninsula. The peninsula's outer coast is indented with fjords and bays among the most isolated in Alaska.

On the mainland opposite the Chugach group lies Port Chatham. At Chrome, on a small bay off Port Chatham, miners sought to develop a chromium mine in the early years of the twentieth century. During World War I about 2,000 tons of the mineral were extracted from the Chrome Bay area. World War II again brought shortages of chromium. This time miners developed the Red Mountain chromium deposit about 12 miles east of Claim Point, the original mine.

Farther north on the coast, Port Graham cuts into the peninsula. The small fishing community of English Bay (population 124), once a Russian trading post known as Alexandrovsk, lies at the bay's southern entrance. Farther into the fjord and connected to English Bay by a four-mile foot trail, is the settlement of Port Graham (population 161). The town grew up around a cannery that today is used as a processing facility to freeze salmon.

Largest community on Kachemak Bay's southern shore is Seldovia (population 505), 16 miles southwest of Homer. Fishing, fish processing, logging, and tourism stir the economy of this town that can be reached only by air or sea. The Alaska Marine Highway ferry on the southwest Alaska

---

Right — *A deserted cabin at Portlock overlooks Port Chatham, 16 miles south of Seldovia. The village, once a cannery site, was named for Capt. Nathaniel Portlock, a British explorer who, along with Capt. George Dixon, visited Cook Inlet in 1786.* (Betty Johannsen, reprinted from *ALASKA GEOGRAPHIC®*)

Right — *Sergius Moonin is the lay priest and reader for the Russian Orthodox Church at English Bay which also serves nearby Port Graham.* (John Jonas)

Below — *Seldovia in 1933 was a cannery town — active in the summer, dormant in the winter. The town was first reported in 1880 as a small settlement of Native sea otter hunters. The first salmon cannery in Seldovia was built in 1910; in 1920 the first recorded processing of king crab took place here. By the mid-1920s, fur farming briefly took the lead as the basis of the town's economy, with 50 mink and fox farms reported in the area.* (Alaska Historical Library)

Rivers and streams of the Kenai Peninsula attract more sport fishermen than any other area in Alaska. Depending on the stream and the season, the catch may include Dolly Varden, steelhead, rainbow trout, or any of several species of salmon.
(Alissa Crandall)

Right — *An orange sea star is examined by Deborah Klein, of Homer, before being returned to the productive waters of China Poot Bay, on Kachemak Bay nine miles southeast of Homer.* (Robert & Janet Klein)

Below — *A tour boat passes Gull Island, in Kachemak Bay.* (Betty Johannsen, reprinted from *ALASKA GEOGRAPHIC®*)

Above — *Razor clams spawn in Cook Inlet from mid-July to mid-September. When a female clam reaches five years or older, she can lay between 15 and 59 million eggs. The larvae float at first, but after several months they sink to the sand and start forming a shell.* (Jim Rearden, staff, reprinted from *ALASKA GEOGRAPHIC®*)

Below — *This black-eyed, masked fellow is Scrape, a friendly harbor seal that welcomes visitors to Halibut Cove.* (John & Margaret Ibbotson)

Above — *Octopus are welcome inhabitants of Kachemak Bay, whose residents use the creatures for food and fish bait.* (Nancy Simmerman, reprinted from *ALASKA GEOGRAPHIC®*)

Right — *Three major species of crab found in Cook Inlet are, from left, king, tanner, and Dungeness.* (Nancy Simmerman, reprinted from *ALASKA GEOGRAPHIC®*)

Far right — *Artist Diana Tillion displays work in progress in her studio at Halibut Cove. The unfinished painting depicts a famous old Cook Inlet tender, the* Celtic. (Jim Rearden, staff)

run calls at the port, which has sheltered vessels of many cultures for centuries. Pacific Eskimos, Aleut hunters, and Tanaina Indians knew of Seldovia Bay, as did the Russians who came to the area in 1792.

Kachemak Bay, 8 miles wide and 40 miles long, arches northeast to the Fox River Delta. Deep fjords and steep, forested slopes characterize much of the bay's southern shore. Small settlements lie tucked away in the bays, icy fingers of glaciers approach tidewater. Boat traffic crosses the bay from Homer on the north shore to Halibut Cove, China Poot Bay, Bear Cove, and other isolated spots on the south shore.

Waterfront homes and warehouses hug the shoreline of Halibut Cove, a community of about 60 permanent residents. The popular recreational area swells to more than 120 residents in summer. Fishermen and artists form the nucleus of the community where travel is by boat, and every family owns at least one, often more. The octopus might well be the cove symbol, for not only is it eaten or used as fish bait by many residents, but Diana Tillion, a nationally recognized artist and cove resident for almost 30 years, finds octopus ink an excellent medium with which to paint.

Kachemak Bay State Park and Kachemak Bay State Wilderness Park, both on the bay's southern shore, offer mountainous terrain, close-up views of glaciers, and beaches rich in scenery and wildlife. Kachemak waters shelter all species of Pacific salmon; numerous species of bottomfish; king, tanner, and Dungeness crab; and five species of shrimp. Marine mammals — seals, porpoises, sea otters, sea lions, beluga whales, killer whales, and some species of great whales — ply these waters.

The bay nourishes a great abundance of marine life because of the propitious mixing of minerals and sunlight, shuffled by currents, and because of water temperatures that are slightly warmer than those of Cook Inlet. These conditions create an optimum environment in which shellfish

Left — *A lush spruce forest grows near Kachemak Bay. White spruce is the Cook Inlet area's most important tree in terms of commercial value.* (Nancy Simmerman, reprinted from *ALASKA GEOGRAPHIC®*)

Above — *Two young subsistence fishermen untangle a salmon from their net along the northern shore of Kachemak Bay. Late summer runs of pink and coho salmon provide a winter supply of protein for many residents.* (Robert & Janet Klein)

larvae and other marine life can thrive. This Eden is enhanced by four-and-a-half-mile-long Homer Spit, which juts out nearly halfway across the bay from its base below the benchland on which present-day Homer sits. The spit restricts the bay's currents and provides calmer waters on the north shore in which intertidal life can flourish.

Seven miles inland from Fox River, Bradley Lake dumps its outflow into Bradley River for the run to Kachemak Bay. In late 1982 state and federal authorities were working on plans to develop a dam at Bradley Lake to supply electrical needs for the Kenai Peninsula.

Kingpin of Kachemak Bay communities is Homer (population about 2,500) on the bay's north shore. The town began on or near Homer Spit when enterprising miners sought to take advantage of nearby coal deposits.

Alaska's coal deposits were first noted by explorers in 1786 near Port Graham. Not much was done with the discovery until 1851, when a Russian mining engineer, Peter Doroshin, was sent to examine seams at Port Graham and other discoveries in Cook Inlet. He returned to Russia in 1853 and urged the Russian-American Company to develop

In 1906, the tiny community of Homer perched at the tip of Homer Spit. Coal and gold mining endeavors in the area had ceased by this time, and the population declined. In the early 1920s, several families of fishermen settled in Homer and their success aroused the interest of homesteaders. Today, fishing remains the backbone of Homer's economy.
(Anchorage Historical & Fine Arts Museum)

the Port Graham coal beds. The mine was a financial disaster, however, and was abandoned in 1865.

In the 1890s, renewed interest in coal stirred activity on Kachemak Bay's northern shore. Miners turned their attention to the scant coal beds east of Homer Spit. These attempts were short-lived, and by 1897 the first two coal companies had ceased operation. A year earlier, however, Homer Pennock, who would give his name to modern-day Homer, had arrived off Homer Spit. Pennock and his men sought gold not coal, but their numbers dwindled as reports of rich gold strikes elsewhere in the territory and the Yukon reached Kachemak Bay. By 1899, when Cook Inlet Coal Fields Company was incorporated, the tiny community was

Paris has its Eiffel Tower, Seattle its Space Needle, and Homer its spit, all four and a half miles of it. The first residents to come to Kachemak Bay's northern shore in modern times settled on or near the spit in the late 19th century. A few years later, Homer Pennock and his crew anchored their boat off the spit before beginning to mine in the area. Their mining endeavors failed, but Homer did give his name to the future town.
(Third Eye Photography)

stagnating. In 1900, the company built the first official town of Homer and set about mining the rich coal seams near Bluff Point, west of the present townsite. In 1902, this company also folded, and Homer languished.

In the second decade of the twentieth century, fox farming, fish processing on the bay's southern shore, and the availability of coal for local use brought about a resurgence of Kachemak Bay settlement.

Great herring runs drew in their wake the fishermen and processors whose livelihood depended on the swarms of small fish. Halibut Cove was founded on the herring runs. Seldovia maintained its preeminence among bay communities because of fish. In addition to packing salmon and herring, Seldovia processors made the first recorded efforts to process king crab in 1920. The herring fishery peaked in the late 1920s, but fox farming had spread around the bay. Farmers raised or trapped red foxes and blue-phase arctic foxes whose pelts were highly valued. In the 1920s and 1930s, fox farming in southcentral Alaska centered around Kachemak Bay. The Great Depression and collapse of the fur market signaled the end of the lucrative industry.

Above — *You've heard of the big fish that got away. This halibut, weighing between 200 and 300 pounds at the Homer dock, is the size of which fish yarns are made. Pacific halibut, largest of several species of flatfish, range from California to the Bering Sea. Females, larger than males, may reach eight feet in length and tip the scales at 500 pounds.* (Third Eye Photography)

Right — *A hose-and-shovel sprinkler sprays water over a shrimp catch to keep it cool and moist on a Homer dock. About five million pounds of shrimp were taken from Kachemak Bay in 1981.* (Vincent McClelland)

Left — *Common murres perch on the rocks above Kachemak Bay.*
(Jim Rearden, staff)

Below — *Hundreds of thousands of shorebirds pass through lower Cook Inlet annually en route to nesting grounds. This surfbird, in winter plumage, stops briefly in Kachemak Bay.* (Norma Dudiak)

Ice clogs the Homer small-boat harbor in early spring.
(Jim Rearden, staff)

Turkeys and geese are just one clue to the subsistence lifestyle of the residents of Nikolaevsk, founded by Old Believers near Anchor Point. (Chlaus Lotscher)

Not until the 1950s, when Homer was connected to Anchorage and the rest of Alaska by the Sterling Highway, did its fishing industry attain solid footing. This, coupled with damage to docks and fish processing facilities at Seldovia from the 1964 earthquake, thrust Homer into the number one position among Kachemak Bay communities. Homer had grown slowly in the years since the coal miners arrived. Many homesteaders drifted in. Farming was tried, but showed little profit. A dock at the end of Homer Spit was built, destroyed, and rebuilt many times. Homer did not boom, but it did grow slowly and inexorably. Today, Homer is the fastest-growing community on the Kenai Peninsula, a focal point for tourism, a haven for artists and retired people, and a thriving fishing port.

With the exception of the Kenai River and its tributary, the Russian, the Anchor River draws the greatest number of sports fishermen in the state, primarily on the four weekends in early summer when king salmon are running. Between 15% and 40% of the total statewide steelhead catch per year comes from Anchor River. Although the runs have been strong for many years, severe flooding on the river in 1979 and 1980 may cause lower returns starting about 1984 and continuing for several years.

With the 1867 purchase of Alaska by the United States, the Russians, who had occupied coastal Alaska since about 1743, departed leaving only a few place names and a few pockets of settlers in Cook Inlet. Russian interest in the Kenai Peninsula came full circle when, 100 years later, a small group of Old Believers, whose ancestors refused to accept reforms to the rites of Russian Orthodoxy, returned to begin the village of Nikolaevsk, inland from Anchor Point, and a new life on the lower peninsula.

In recent years, some Nikolaevsk residents have felt the encroachment of modern culture and have moved to the

Above — *Members of a younger generation of Old Believers pose for photographer Marian Rohrbeck at Nikolaevsk. About 13 years ago, a small contingent of Old Believers, refugees from Russian Orthodoxy whose ancestors refused to accept reforms of traditional rites, came to the lower peninsula to establish a new community near Anchor Point.*

Upper right — *Cooper Landing residents Angela Mantzoros (left) and Mary Anne Walker show off some of the rabbits they raise for food and fur.* (Tom Walker)

Right — *The rat game is a popular attraction at the Kenai Peninsula state fair at Ninilchik. Two rats, released on the center white spot, scamper around the table top until one disappears through the hole on a colored section. People with quarter bets on that color double their money; those with bets on a different color lose.* (Robert & Janet Klein)

head of Kachemak Bay to set up a new community, Kachemak Selo. Access to the village, as of summer 1982, was only by boat or travel along the beach.

"Biggest Little Fair in Alaska" claim Ninilchik residents for their late-summer get-together. But when the frolicking is over, people here look to fish for their economic survival. Two facilities, a processing plant for salmon and a receiving station, handle the majority of the catch. Fish are brought in from nearby waters to this port about 37 miles north of Homer. Beaches around Ninilchik are good for beach-combing and clamming. Symbol of the community may be the Russian Orthodox Church, which sits on the bluff over-looking the town.

Travelers following the Sterling Highway north from Homer enjoy some of the most spectacular vistas in a spectacular land. Across Cook Inlet rise Mount Iliamna (10,016 feet) and Mount Redoubt (10,197 feet), and other Aleutian Range peaks, snow-capped year-round. Ocean freighters pass through the inlet on their way to or from Anchorage or Kenai. Oil tankers head for Cook Inlet rigs near The Forelands or for oil-related facilities at Kenai and Nikiski. The broad, sandy beaches below are alive with clam-diggers

Left — *Evening light creates a tranquil scene at Skilak Lake, 27 miles southeast of Kenai. But this moment of calm can be deceiving, for powerful winds sometimes sweep across Skilak Glacier and roar down the Skilak River Valley, swiftly creating dangerous conditions for boaters.* (David Westerman)

Above — *With the first minus tides of spring, thousands of clam-crazy Cook Inletters swarm to the beaches along the eastern shore, primarily south of Kenai River to Kachemak Bay. Others take boats or small planes across Cook Inlet to the clam-rich beaches near Polly Creek.* (Mark Kelley, reprinted from *ALASKA GEOGRAPHIC®*)

Below — *Fishing boats line the dock at Ninilchik. The town, with a 1980 population of 341, was first settled by employees of the Russian-American Company in the early 1800s.* (Dan Kowalski, reprinted from *ALASKA GEOGRAPHIC®*)

Right — *Fort Saint Nicholas, built by Grigor Konovalov in 1791, was the second permanent Russian settlement in Alaska. This shrine, long out of use, is one of several attractions in the Kenai area.* (Jim Thiele, reprinted from *ALASKA GEOGRAPHIC®*)

Below — *Fort Kenai (or Kenay) was built by the U.S. Army in 1869, one of six army posts established after the United States purchase of Alaska. The fort occupied the same site at the mouth of the Kenai River as Redoubt Saint Nicholas, a trading post built by the Russians in 1791. Today, the Kenai Historical Society has constructed a replica of the fort's log barracks, and operates a museum at the site.* (U.S. Signal Corps, photo no. 111-SC-87815 in the National Archives)

seeking tasty razor clams, and with set netters and small-boat fishermen when the salmon are running.

Several hatcheries contribute fish to Cook Inlet runs. At Kasilof, 64 miles north of Homer, the Crooked Creek hatchery raises sockeye salmon and is experimenting with nurturing young king salmon. Tutka Bay hatchery, between Seldovia and Halibut Cove, raises stocks of pink and a few chum salmon. This hatchery produced 65% of the pink salmon harvest for lower Cook Inlet in 1981. The entire 1982 harvest of 2,500 king salmon taken at Halibut Cove was hatchery-raised fish.

Kenai (population about 4,500) and its neighbor, Soldotna (population about 2,400) form the largest metropolitan complex on the peninsula. Discovery of oil 20 miles northwest of Kenai near Swanson River and gas near Kalifonsky two years later brought the trappings of mainstream America to Kenai. But as a trading center, Kenai has a long tradition stretching back more than two centuries. Even before the Russians arrived in southcentral Alaska, early Indians traded from this site where the Kenai River flows into Cook Inlet. When the Russians came in 1791, they established their second permanent settlement in North America here with construction of Saint Nicholas Redoubt.

Miners, trappers, homesteaders, and fishermen gradually settled the Kenai area pursuing a subsistence and small-town lifestyle until the tidal wave of oil activity thrust the area into the limelight.

In addition to the Swanson River discoveries, oil had been found offshore in the Middle Ground Shoals, and at McArthur River, Granite Point, and Trading Bay in upper Cook Inlet. Here 13 platforms pump oil and one draws natural gas from beneath Cook Inlet. The raw materials

Left — *This close-up photo of the corner of the shrine at Fort Saint Nicholas shows the builder's careful attention to detail.* (Nancy Simmerman, reprinted from *ALASKA GEOGRAPHIC®*)

Above — *Each spring thousands of snow geese arrive at the Kenai Flats near the mouth of the Kenai River on their annual migration to breeding grounds farther north. Many fly as far as Wrangel Island off the Soviet Union's northern coast to nest.* (Helen Rhode)

Below — *Conor Mullen, four, shows off the present he is taking to a friend's birthday party. Behind him are the chicken coop and greenhouse tended by his parents, Janis and Frank Mullen of Soldotna.* (Virginia McKinney, staff)

Left — *This photo shows 4 of the 13 oil rigs currently operating in upper Cook Inlet. Pipelines carry oil and gas to shoreline plants and loading docks.* (Nancy Simmerman, reprinted from *ALASKA GEOGRAPHIC®*)

Below — *A Cook Inlet rig tender battles to stay alongside in a stiff tide.* (Nancy Simmerman, reprinted from *ALASKA GEOGRAPHIC®*)

An escape module from a Mobil Oil platform undergoes its annual test. Accidental dunkings in Cook Inlet are to be avoided at all costs — the currents are swift and the waters cold. (Anthony Flora, reprinted from *ALASKA GEOGRAPHIC®*)

Left — *Fishing boats anchor in the Kenai River near canneries at the Port of Kenai. About 15 processors freeze, smoke, or can fish, primarily salmon, at Kenai.* (Jon Nickles)

Above — *Setting the night sky ablaze, Union Oil's chemical plant at Nikiski, just north of Kenai, gives dramatic testament to the area's industrial base. The plant produces urea and ammonia which are used for fertilizer.* (Jon Nickles)

flow through underground pipes to onshore storage and shipping facilities.

North of town toward Nikiski and North Kenai, industrial giants such as Union Oil Company and Chevron USA operate oil refineries and produce oil and gas and by-products such as ammonia and urea used for fertilizer. Phillips Petroleum operates the country's only liquefied natural gas plant here. The plant's entire output is shipped to Japan.

Tourism and salmon fishing and processing make up the remainder of Kenai's economic base. Fish processing is big business in the Kenai-Soldotna-Kasilof area where at least 15 proc-essors freeze, smoke, or can fish, mostly salmon. One small facility processes clams.

Soldotna, east of Kenai, grew up around the junction of the Sterling Highway and Kenai Spur Road. Today it is a thriving commercial center, seat of government for Kenai Peninsula Borough, and headquarters for Kenai National Wildlife Refuge. Almost two million acres of the Kenai Penin-sula are included in the refuge, part

of which was set aside in 1941 to preserve habitat for the peninsula's famed moose. These large members of the deer family are not the only animals to take advantage of the refuge's habitat: Dall sheep and mountain goats inhabit mountainous regions, two small herds of caribou roam the interior, black and brown/grizzly bears, lynx, wolves, coyotes, smaller mammals, and 146 species of resident and migratory birds share the terrain. Waterfowl congregate at Chickaloon Flats along Turnagain Arm at the refuge's northernmost reach. Nine river systems drain the refuge, several of which originate at glaciers in the Harding Icefield atop the Kenai Mountains. Approximately 40% of the catch taken by Cook Inlet commercial fishermen spawn in refuge waters.

From Soldotna, the Sterling Highway leaves Cook Inlet and heads east across the Kenai Peninsula to the Kenai

Left — *Kenai National Wildlife Refuge covers nearly two million acres of land, lakes, and rivers. The refuge has become a popular spot for hikers, sport fishermen, cross-country skiers, and kayakers.* (Nancy Simmerman, reprinted from *ALASKA GEOGRAPHIC®*)

Above — *The best place in the Cook Inlet area to find moose is probably the Kenai National Wildlife Refuge, which provides almost two million acres of ideal habitat.*
(John & Margaret Ibbotson, reprinted from *ALASKA GEOGRAPHIC®*)

Right — *The lynx population follows the ups and downs of the snowshoe hare, its favorite food.* (John S. Crawford, reprinted from *ALASKA GEOGRAPHIC®*)

This locomotive and car of the Alaska Railroad, one of the lifelines connecting the widely separated communities of Cook Inlet basin, cross the Twentymile Valley near Portage. The line hauls freight from its southern terminus at Seward north to Anchorage and on to Fairbanks; except for charters, passengers are carried only from Portage north to Fairbanks. A spur line moves passengers and freight along the Portage Creek Valley and through two tunnels to Whittier on Prince William Sound. (Penny Rennick, staff)

Above — *Cook Inlet basin is home for a number of species of small mammals, such as this hoary marmot.* (John & Margaret Ibbotson, reprinted from *ALASKA GEOGRAPHIC*®)

Right — *A bull caribou stands at attention among fall-colored foliage. Two herds of caribou make their home on the Kenai Peninsula.* (John & Margaret Ibbotson, reprinted from *ALASKA GEOGRAPHIC*®)

Rugged, treeless peaks, many crowned by glaciers or snowfields, define the eastern and southern Kenai Peninsula boundaries. This hunter (left) surveys the forested valley and bare, rocky slopes of the Kenai Mountains northwest of Seward. By contrast, much of the western and northern peninsula is flat land, broken by low, rolling hills, and crisscrossed by rivers, lakes, and ponds. Northeast of Kenai, two canoe trail systems, Swanson River and Swan Lake, connect lakes and rivers in a watery maze. This family (below) explores the Swan Lake system. (Both by Will Troyer)

Mountains. Low, rolling hills blanketed with spruce and deciduous forests characterize the area. North of the highway, the 80-mile Swanson River Canoe Route connects 40 lakes with the Swanson River. Not to be confused with the Swanson River trail is the Swan Lake Canoe Route, which links 30 lakes with branches of the Moose River. For those who like to catch their supper, Dolly Varden, rainbow trout, and coho salmon inhabit most lakes along the Swan Lake route. In May and June, cow moose come to the northern peninsula lakes region to have their calves. Common loons, other species of waterfowl, and beavers take advantage of the watery habitat to raise their young.

The land rises toward the eastern side of the peninsula where the mountains block moisture from the sea, and many peaks are buried in snowfields. The Kenai River, 75 miles long, drains Kenai Lake before the trek across the lowlands to Cook Inlet. Huge Kenai Lake stretches out in a modified S-shape 24 miles from Cooper Landing at the outlet to the Kenai River on the west to the mouth of Snow River on the south. About 100 people live in Cooper Landing, most by subsistence or by servicing traffic on the Sterling Highway. The Kenai River has some of the best-known fishing in southcentral Alaska. Each summer fishermen gather here to try their luck with the salmon. South-facing slopes of mountains just to the north are prime lambing habitat for Dall sheep.

Most activity in the eastern peninsula takes place in the valleys . . . hikers trek the valleys, moose browse in the valleys, miners stake claims in the valleys. Sometimes these multiple interests compete for land, and forest service officials must decide how to accommodate conflicting claims. For instance, where Crescent Creek flows into Quartz Creek east of Cooper Landing, active mines, a proposed access to undeveloped mining claims, and popular recreation trails all use the same valley.

At Tern Lake, the Sterling Highway joins the Seward Highway reaching between Anchorage and Seward on Resurrection Bay. Moose Pass, a tiny community of 76 residents, lines both sides of the highway as it skirts the west shore of Upper Trail Lake. Several lakes and rivers flow into the valley as the highway makes its run to Seward. A fish hatchery at Upper Trail Lake began raising sockeye salmon

and a few coho and king salmon in 1982. Closer to Seward, an eight-mile road has been opened to Exit Glacier, one of 15 rivers of ice that flow from Harding Icefield in Kenai Fjords National Park. By summer 1983 National Park Service officials hope to have a visitor center with scheduled hikes from the end of the road two miles up the valley to the base of the glacier.

Formerly a busy fishing and shipping port, the fortunes of Seward changed drastically after the 1964 earthquake destroyed many of the harbor facilities and 90% of the town's economy. But Seward is tough, and the community of nearly 2,000 that got its start as the tidewater terminus for the Alaska Central Railroad in 1902 is bouncing back.

In the 1970s, Seward sought to diversify its economy. Tourism, timber, fishing, and government generated some revenue. Still, unemployment, especially in winter, plagued

Seward got its start in 1902, when the Alaska Central Railroad leased land from homesteaders on Resurrection Bay. In August 1903 the first permanent settlers arrived, and buildings began going up immediately. The railroad went bankrupt in 1906, and by the time this photo was taken, in 1907 or 1908, the busy little town had become dormant. Construction on the railroad began again around 1909, and the town prospered. In late 1918 the railroad between Seward and Anchorage was completed, and Seward became established as a terminal port.
(Anchorage Historical & Fine Arts Museum)

the community. By the 1980s, Seward residents were determined to push for a new industrial marine complex. At Fourth of July Creek, across Resurrection Bay from the town proper, developers have altered the creek bed and completed groundwork for construction of a new harbor facility. Work began in January 1982 to dredge the harbor and construct a breakwater, and a shiplift pier. In its initial stages, the complex will focus on ship repair and fabrication. City officials have planned expansion to accommodate new industries coming into the area.

There is more to Seward than just the industrial complex. A fishing fleet calls the town its home port, and the small boat harbor shelters many recreational craft. Seward officials hope a grain terminal to handle crops produced in interior Alaska will be built on Resurrection Bay.

Seward Fisheries cans salmon, halibut, and crab and processes herring roe. At their by-products plant, which can handle 150 tons of raw material every 24 hours, they produce herring meal and oil, salmon meal and oil, crab meal, and Mushers Mix, a ration designed for sled and other working dogs. Other processors in Seward salt herring roe and freeze salmon. The University of Alaska maintains a marine laboratory near the ferry slip where Alaska Marine Highway ferries dock. Some freight is offloaded at Seward for shipment north on the Alaska Railroad.

The town is headquarters for Kenai Fjords National Park. Boat excursions to the Chiswell Islands, just outside the park, and to fjords along the peninsula's outer coast bring close-up looks at Steller sea lions, sea otters, black-legged kittiwakes, common murres, and puffin rookeries, and tidewater glaciers. Flightseeing trips circle over Harding Icefield for panoramic views of icy fingers clutching the land.

Left — *Seward (population 1,943) stretches along the coast of Resurrection Bay, at the foot of 4,603-foot Mount Marathon. The town was named for Secretary of State William H. Seward, who was instrumental in arranging the purchase of Alaska from Russia in 1867.* (Tom Walker)

Above — *Longtime Alaskans Eva Culverson (left), Walter and Vivian Teeland, and Jasmine Pickett, representing the Pioneer Igloo Auxiliaries, wave to the crowd during the Fourth of July parade at Seward.* (Alissa Crandall)

Left — *Deep fjords and rugged shorelines characterize the Kenai Peninsula's outer coast. Offshore, a few, steep-sloped islands take the full brunt of the Gulf of Alaska's relentless pounding. Outer Island, shown here with the mainland in the distance, is part of the Pye Island group on the east side of Nuka Bay.* (Don Cornelius)

Above — *A bull Steller sea lion bellows his superiority while pups gather around a disinterested female at this rookery on the Pye Islands along the Kenai Peninsula's outer coast. These marine mammals, largest of the eared seals, range from extreme southeastern Alaska to the Bering Sea.* (Don Cornelius)

Right — *A hiker cautiously crosses the outlet to Delight Lake near the East Arm of Nuka Bay on the Kenai Peninsula's outer coast.* (Don Cornelius)

The Kenai Peninsula is attached to the remainder of Alaska by a slender isthmus stretching from Turnagain Arm to Passage Canal on Prince William Sound. Portage, at the head of the arm, is a stop for the Alaska Railroad on its run north from Seward to Anchorage. From here a spur extends 12.5 miles along Portage Creek Valley and through two tunnels to Whittier on Passage Canal. Much of the land near Portage sank during the 1964 earthquake, and vegetation was killed by incoming salt water.

Portage Glacier and Lake are among the state's top 10 tourist attractions. Icebergs float up and down the lake,

sometimes crowding the shoreline in front of the visitor center. For centuries overland travelers crossed the glacier on journeys from Cook Inlet to Prince William Sound. In the late 1800s, the glacier reached much farther into Portage Creek Valley, but by 1914, with retreat of the glacier, the beginnings of Portage Lake had been exposed. A century later, by the 1980s, Portage Glacier had receded more than two miles.

Chugach State Park draws adventurous cross-country hikers and weekend walkers to the high alpine country of the Chugach Mountains southeast of Anchorage. Mountain climbing, long distance trekking, berry picking, hang gliding, cross-country skiing, gold panning . . . just about any form of outdoor recreation that can be imagined has been tried in the park. A major resort has been developed at Alyeska, 40 miles south of Anchorage, where world class downhill skiing is the big draw.

Across Turnagain Arm the small mining communities of Hope and Sunrise stand as relics of Kenai Peninsula's mining past. A resurgence of mining has stirred the sleepy communities, and paving of the road leading from the Seward Highway down Sixmile Creek Valley to the settlements along the Turnagain shoreline has made it easier for Anchorage residents to spend weekends at these historical retreats.

Left — *A favorite pastime for travelers along the Seward Highway is watching the bore tide roar up Turnagain Arm. These spectacular tides are formed when flood tides are forced into a constricted inlet. One- to two-foot bores are common in Turnagain Arm, but spring tides may push the bore up to six feet or more.* (Third Eye Photography)

Above — *Framed by a frozen wave of ice, a cross-country skier winds his way across Portage Lake.* (Jim Burkholder)

Above — *A weary hiker pauses at the top of Wolverine Peak (4,455 feet) southeast of Anchorage in Chugach State Park.* (Betty Johannsen, reprinted from *ALASKA GEOGRAPHIC®*)

Left — *Helicopter skiing is an exciting outdoor sport available in the Anchorage area. These skiers are in the Chugach Mountains, southeast of Anchorage.* (Nancy Simmerman, reprinted from *ALASKA GEOGRAPHIC®*)

Left — *Alyeska Resort, with snow from November to May, offers spectacular chairlift rides three-fourths of the way to the top of 3,939-foot Mount Alyeska. In the background is Turnagain Arm; also visible is the Seward Highway.* (Susan Hackley Johnson, reprinted from *ALASKA GEOGRAPHIC®*)

Below — *A cold winter's light casts a golden glow over snowy and slippery Turnagain Pass, six miles south of Turnagain Arm on the route from Anchorage to the Kenai Peninsula.* (Third Eye Photography)

Right — *A small herd of cattle keep watch while Carl Clark of Hope takes time out to pet a young moose that he is helping to raise.* (Helen Rhode)

Some straw playmates lean against the schoolhouse at Hope, a small mining community and weekend retreat for Anchorage residents on the south side of Turnagain Arm. (Freda Shen)

The Matanuska-Susitna Valley

Two major rivers give their name to the Mat-Su region north of Anchorage. To the east of Anchorage, at the head of Knik Arm, the Matanuska River dumps its silty glacial water into Cook Inlet. The mighty Susitna River, 260 miles long, flows into the inlet about 24 miles west of Anchorage. These two drainages form the major watershed for a region of meandering streams, countless ponds, rich lowlands with active and future agricultural promise, topped by the Talkeetna Mountains, and bordered by the Alaska Range on the west and north, and the Chugach Range on the east and south.

Palmer (population 2,275) and Wasilla (population 1,928) serve as administrative and commercial centers for the Mat-Su. Palmer resembles a small agricultural community typical of the Midwest. But the towering mountains surrounding the community are not at all reminiscent of the Great Plains. Palmer takes its name from an early trader,

A farmer cuts hay on his property in the Matanuska Valley. Rich soil and long summer days create an ideal agricultural environment in the valley, where crop value in 1981 was $4.3 million. (Third Eye Photography)

106

Above — *This short-season hybrid corn grows at the University of Alaska's Experimental Farm, near Palmer. Although the plants are only three to four feet tall, they have produced mature ears.* (Nancy Simmerman, reprinted from *ALASKA GEOGRAPHIC®*)

Right — *Pioneer Peak (6,398 feet), a local landmark, rises above a sign announcing Hamilton Farms, Inc. The farm is the largest of eight producing dairy farms which are part of Matanuska Maid, a farmers' cooperative which supplies dairy products to area residents.* (Third Eye Photography)

The Glenn Highway, covered with November ice, winds
through bare trees near Sutton, 20 miles northeast of Palmer.
Sutton was founded about 1918 as an Alaska Railroad station
serving the nearby coal fields. Today, the community has a
population of about 180. (Pete Martin)

George Palmer, who grew vegetables near the shore of Knik Arm in one of the first attempts to bring agriculture to a valley that would become known as Alaska's food basket. When the federal government in the 1930s sought to restore confidence in the country during the Great Depression, officials bugled the call of the frontier and imported people from the Lower 48 to colonize the Matanuska Valley, a 60-mile lowland of rich soil and long summer days.

State officials hope to expand agricultural output from the Matanuska Valley, which in 1981 amounted to nearly $4.3 million worth of crops and $3.3 million worth of livestock and poultry. Farmers have had to contend with surburban creep from Anchorage and growing industry and commerce which has chipped away at the land available for agri-

culture. To spur additional output, officials auctioned 13,940 acres of land at Point MacKenzie, across Knik Arm from Anchorage, for future agricultural development in September 1982.

Knik and the area along Knik Arm's north shore had been a commercial center since the earliest days of settlement in the Matanuska Valley. When the George Parks Highway opened a new link between Anchorage and Fairbanks in 1972, the tiny community of Wasilla spread along the junction of Knik Road and the Parks Highway.

Knik Arm itself impedes expansion of metropolitan Anchorage to the north in the same way that the Chugach Range blocks its growth to the east and south. During the past several decades, proposals have been put forth for

Above — *This abandoned building stands in the ghost town of Matanuska, a few miles southwest of Palmer. Matanuska was established in 1915 as an Alaska Railroad station.* (Staff)

Upper right — *Wasilla Lake, just east of the community of Wasilla, is a popular spot for swimmers, boaters, and sunbathers.* (Polly Walter, staff)

Right — *False fronts adorn this Wasilla shopping center, lending a Western flavor. Wasilla is a growing town located about an hour's drive north of Anchorage. In July 1981 the town boasted a population of almost 2,000.* (Tom Walker)

Right — *A trio watches for geese in the Matanuska Valley.* (Nancy Simmerman, reprinted from *ALASKA GEOGRAPHIC®*)

Below — *A group of rafters hits a stretch of choppy water on the Matanuska River.* (John & Margaret Ibbotson)

Geometric fields in the Matanuska Valley offer a sharp contrast to the irregular form of massive Knik Glacier, in the distance. (Nancy Simmerman, reprinted from *ALASKA GEOGRAPHIC®*)

Left — *The craggy blue terminus of Matanuska Glacier, located about 100 miles northeast of Anchorage along the Glenn Highway. The glacier drains into the Matanuska River.*
(Bill Devine)

Right — *Knik Arm, north of Anchorage, is a 40-mile-long muddy inlet. Knik River and Matanuska River flow into the head of the arm, a popular waterfowl-hunting area. This view is from the west side of lower Knik Arm, looking north.*
(John & Margaret Ibbotson, reprinted from *ALASKA GEOGRAPHIC®*)

building a crossing of Knik Arm. Causeways, bridges, tunnels . . . the schemes have been many, but cost, tides, earthquakes, ice, and numerous other obstacles have forced delay or dismissal of these projects. In 1983 state administrators are once again considering a crossing of the arm, a step which would cut miles off the journey from Anchorage to the Parks Highway.

As an adjunct to a vehicular crossing, European and American developers have proposed harnessing the extreme tides which rake the arm. These suggestions call for using tidal energy to generate power for Anchorage and railbelt communities along the Alaska Railroad right of way north from Anchorage. Two sites along Knik Arm — Point MacKenzie and near Eagle Bay — and a third site along Turnagain Arm have been determined by the most recent study to have suitable conditions for building and operating a tidal power plant.

How Tidal Power Plants Work

Editor's note: *This material is adapted from* The Susitna Hydro Studies, *April 1982, courtesy of the Alaska Power Authority.*

The need for electrical power is generally dictated by when people use it. Unfortunately, tidal power is only produced with high and low cycles of the tide. These do not always coincide with normal morning and evening peak demand periods. Available water pressure also varies from day to day and season to season.

To efficiently harness tidal power, a dam is built across a bay or estuary to impound sea water in a basin. The enclosed basin fills during the incoming tide. When the tide reaches its highest level, all gates are closed. The out-going tide recedes, causing a pressure differential between the sea and the impounded sea water. Sea water from the basin is then allowed to run out to sea through the turbine

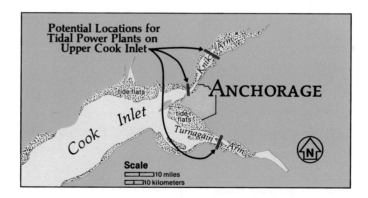

generators. This type of tidal plant uses sea flow in one direction and is called a single effect tidal plant. Double effect tidal plants use tidal power in both directions. A third type of plant is capable of storing energy until needed.

Left — *Knik Glacier, whose craggy terminus is shown here, is one of many glaciers found in the Chugach Mountains. In the background are Inner Lake George and Colony Glacier.* (Nancy Simmerman, reprinted from *ALASKA GEOGRAPHIC®*)

Below — *The Glenn Highway and Alaska Railroad cut straight paths across the Matanuska and Knik rivers, about 10 miles southwest of Palmer.* (Jon Nickles)

Right — *A calm pond is framed by trees along the Knik River Road, with the Talkeetna Mountains in the background.* (John & Margaret Ibbotson)

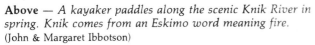

Above — *A kayaker paddles along the scenic Knik River in spring. Knik comes from an Eskimo word meaning fire.* (John & Margaret Ibbotson)

Right — *Grave or spirit houses stand in the cemetery in front of Saint Nicholas Russian Orthodox Church in Eklutna, 16 miles southwest of Palmer. Some of the spirit houses are brightly painted in traditional family colors.* (John & Margaret Ibbotson)

Far right — *A hunter and his Labrador retriever cross Eklutna Flats, near the head of Knik Arm, 25 miles northeast of Anchorage.* (June Mackie, reprinted from *ALASKA*® magazine)

The town of Knik grew up in the late 1800s as a transportation
and distribution center for nearby mining districts. The town
prospered briefly in the early 1900s, with a population
approaching 500. Many of Knik's residents moved to Anchorage
when railroad construction began there in 1915, and gradually
Knik became a ghost town. (Anchorage Historical
& Fine Arts Museum)

Left — *Recently restored Knik Hall is the only structure left of the bustling community of the early 1900s. Knik served as a supply center for the nearby Willow Creek mining district.* (Tom Walker)

Below — *A dog team and sled carrying a load of gold stands outside the Pioneer Roadhouse at Knik in 1916. The town was located along the Iditarod Trail, which served as a winter route to the Iditarod gold fields on the Kuskokwim River. Today, Knik still serves as checkpoint number four on the annual Iditarod Trail Sled Dog Race.* (Anchorage Historical & Fine Arts Museum)

Abundant peat deposits and the potential for hydroelectric and geothermal power make the Susitna Valley an important source of energy to meet the state's future needs. Peat is partially decomposed plant material mixed with minerals in a water-saturated environment. The water hinders decomposition and prevents carbon and oxygen normally given off during biological decomposition from escaping to the surface. Peat deposits occur in initial stages of the long geological process of making coal. In the Susitna Valley, there are about 1.8 million acres of fuel-grade peat, i.e., deposits at least five feet thick and unfrozen. In summer 1983 geologists will explore for more fuel-grade peat deposits near the Beluga area on the west side of Cook Inlet and on the Kenai Peninsula.

Any mention of potential hydroelectric power for Anchorage and the Mat-Su area comes down to one word: Susitna. While the two dams — Watana and Devil Canyon — proposed for the Susitna project would be built on the fringes of Cook Inlet country, their impact on Anchorage and the Cook Inlet basin would be tremendous.

About 118 air miles north of Anchorage, a narrow canyon constricts the Susitna's course, and raging rapids churn the river into a frothing mass of world class whitewater. Kayakers come from several continents to take on the Susitna at Devil Canyon. And not until the 1970s did the first boater survive the 15-mile shoot from the junction of Devil Creek to where the river squirts through what kayakers call the "Pearly Gates," or Gorge Rapids, on its escape from the confining canyon walls.

And it is at this canyon that Alaska Power Authority officials propose to build the second of the two dams comprising the Susitna Hydroelectric Project. Watana, an earth-rockfill dam, is slated to rise about 30 miles upriver from Devil Canyon Dam. With a proposed height of about 880 feet, Watana would be the fifth highest dam in the world and the highest in North America. Behind the dam, water

This typical cross section of a peat deposit shows the definite layers representing various stages in the decomposition process. Geologists have discovered approximately 1.8 million acres of fuel-grade peat in the Susitna Valley, and are extending their exploration to other areas around Cook Inlet. (Don Markle)

The Susitna River, "Big Su," is a 260-mile-long waterway that dominates the Susitna Valley and tests the course-choosing abilities of riverboaters. The meandering river begins high in the Alaska Range. (Sepp Weber, reprinted from ALASKA® magazine)

This NASA high-altitude infrared photo shows a portion of the Susitna Valley, with the Parks Highway running from bottom to top. The road going to the right near the bottom of the photo is Hatcher Pass Road; the town of Willow is at the junction of the two roads. The pinkish area in the center of the photo is Rogers Creek bog, which has been found to be rich in fuel-grade peat deposits. (NASA JSC 406 AUG 79)

Above — *A riverboat plies the calm waters of the Yentna River. From its origin at Yentna Glacier, the river winds gracefully for about 80 miles to where it flows into the Susitna River.* (John & Margaret Ibbotson)

Left — *Dennis McAllister of Alaska Department of Fish & Game draws a blood sample from a tranquilized moose near the mouth of the Susitna River. The sample will be used to determine the general health of the animal, part of ADF&G's program to study the impact of Susitna hydroelectric projects on the area's wildlife.* (Nancy Tankersley)

Alaska Department of Fish & Game employees relax at Susitna Station, headquarters for the department's sonar operations on the lower Susitna River. Sonar is used underwater to monitor fish populations, part of ADF&G's Susitna hydroelectric environmental impact studies. (Stuart Pechek)

Clockwise from above — *A moose feeds on succulent grass from a shallow pond in the late summer. Moose are abundant throughout the Cook Inlet area, from the Kenai Peninsula to the Alaska Range.* (Helen Rhode)

The willow ptarmigan, official state bird, inhabits thickets, tundra, and muskeg throughout the Cook Inlet area. (Helen Rhode)

A black bear wanders through the brush near the Susitna River. (Third Eye Photography, reprinted from *ALASKA GEOGRAPHIC*®)

from the Susitna would form a reservoir 54 miles long. Devil Canyon Dam is planned as a concrete arch structure about 635 feet high with a 28-mile-long reservoir.

Watana and Devil Canyon dams, power houses, access roads, utility lines, and all the other trappings that go with a major hydroelectric project were estimated in fall 1982 to cost $5.1 billion. Estimated capacity is 1,620 megawatts.

The potential for geothermal energy is unknown at this point in the development of the Susitna Valley. University of Alaska scientists believe heated water may have escaped toward the surface from deep within the earth along faults. When the water reached shallow layers of porous sand and gravel, it spread out and formed reservoirs of natural hot water in the valley. Observers report that portions of Nancy Lake, about 30 air miles north of Anchorage, do not freeze over in winter because of upwellings of warm water from the lake bottom. A subsurface temperature of 170° was measured while drilling for oil about seven miles south of

The Alaska Railroad, whose construction created several towns in the Matanuska-Susitna Valley area, presents several excellent views of Mount McKinley as it winds north through the valleys, climbing gradually to Broad Pass in the Alaska Range, then descending into the Interior. (Betty Johannsen, reprinted from *ALASKA GEOGRAPHIC*®)

Willow. This temperature, and the results of a helium soil gas survey — normal air and soil have about five parts per million of helium; when scientists can measure more than this amount of helium, they know some anomaly exists which is pushing helium to the earth's surface — suggest reservoirs of hot water sufficient for heating and for agricultural use, if not for generating electricity.

Miners formed the vanguard for much of the settlement in the Susitna Valley. Fortune seekers pushed up the river and on to the tributaries flowing from the Talkeetna Mountains to the east. Their quest: placer gold. They had found the

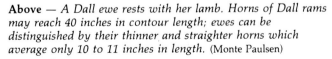

Above — *A Dall ewe rests with her lamb. Horns of Dall rams may reach 40 inches in contour length; ewes can be distinguished by their thinner and straighter horns which average only 10 to 11 inches in length.* (Monte Paulsen)

Right — *Ski instructor Nancy Pfeiffer glides down a slope on Ruth Glacier. In the background, clouds sweep off the summit of Mount McKinley (20,320 feet).* (Jon Fowler)

A climbing group, including two paraplegic members, takes a lunch break in the great gorge of Ruth Glacier, on the south slope of the Alaska Range. The expedition, organized by the Alaska Handicapped Sports and Recreation Association, was the first of its kind. (Jon Fowler)

placer by 1897, and before long they located the primary gold lodes. By 1906, the first hard-rock claim was staked in the Willow Creek district. Soon, miners had tunneled deep into the rugged, gold-bearing mountains, and the mines bore such magical names as Snowbird, Fern, Lucky Shot, Mabel, and War Baby.

But the productive days were short-lived. Even before World War II, unfavorable economics had forced a long closure of some of the mines. This country's entry into the war brought a presidential edict in 1942 closing down all gold mining operations.

In August 1982 Alaska formally recognized the miners' accomplishments by opening Independence Mine State Historic Park in the Hatcher Pass area northwest of Palmer and east of Willow. Between 1936 and 1942, Alaska-Pacific Consolidated Mining Co. — whose mill, camp, and claims form the park's core — drew 140,974 ounces of gold worth almost $5 million from hills surrounding the pass. The company's assay office and manager's house have been restored. The former now contains interpretative exhibits and will be renovated to resemble a working assay office. The manager's house is now the park's visitor center.

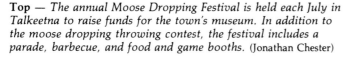

Top — *The annual Moose Dropping Festival is held each July in Talkeetna to raise funds for the town's museum. In addition to the moose dropping throwing contest, the festival includes a parade, barbecue, and food and game booths.* (Jonathan Chester)

Above — *Passengers gather on the platform of the Alaska Railroad station at Talkeetna, a starting point for mountain climbers and river rafters.* (Jerrianne Lowther)

Left — *Shuttle buses ferry visitors from Palmer in the Matanuska Valley (in distance) to the opening of Independence Mine State Historic Park at Hatcher Pass in August 1982. The park, centered around the former mill and camp of Alaska-Pacific Consolidated Mining Co., commemorates the rich gold mining history of the Hatcher Pass area. The former manager's house (left) is now the park's visitor center. In winter, the area is tops for cross-country skiing.* (Penny Rennick, staff)

Below — *A few berries are still visible amid the brilliant red autumn leaves of this highbush cranberry, seen near Byers Lake, north of Talkeetna.* (John & Margaret Ibbotson)

Above — *One of the region's favorite hang-gliding areas is Hatcher Pass, where fliers are treated to ideal takeoff spots, treeless landings, and great scenery.* (Ted Bell, reprinted from *ALASKA GEOGRAPHIC*®)

Below — *In winter and spring Hatcher Pass is a good spot to test snow machines and sled dogs. This team belongs to Joe Redington, Sr., "Father of the Iditarod Race," who lives in Knik.* (Betty Johannsen, reprinted from *ALASKA GEOGRAPHIC*®)

Left — *A skier furrows through a deep blanket of snow in Hatcher Pass, 13 miles northwest of Palmer in the Talkeetna Mountains.* (John W. Warden)

Below — *A camper enjoys the rolling terrain of the Peters Hills area, in the Alaska Range about 25 miles northwest of Talkeetna.* (John & Margaret Ibbotson)

The West Side

If Anchorage represents urban Alaska, the west side of Cook Inlet conjures up images of just the opposite. Wilderness rules the west side . . . towering mountains, active volcanoes, pristine glacial valleys, untrampled beaches . . . and, with the exception of those seeking to develop the region's energy potential, the relatively few human intruders who broach the wall of the Aleutian Range come to fish or hunt.

Today, the only settlement in the narrow coastal strip from the Susitna flats to Cape Douglas is Tyonek, a Tanaina Indian community of 239 about 43 air miles southwest of Anchorage. In the 1700s, the Russians built two trading settlements on the west side, one probably located at Tyonek and another to the south at Iliamna. Dissension between the Russians and Natives brought about destruc-

---

The flat, glacial plain of Cape Douglas was named by Capt. James Cook in honor of his good friend Dr. John Douglas, canon of Windsor. Douglas Glacier spills down from cloud-enshrouded, 7,000-foot Mount Douglas, a slumbering volcanic peak. The cape is part of Katmai National Park and Preserve. (Nina Faust)

Left — *Members of the Klondike & Boston Gold Mining & Manufacturing Company's 4th expedition set up camp on the beach at Tyonek in 1898. Orville G. Herning led the company's efforts which brought out most of the placer gold taken from the Willow Creek district.* (Anchorage Historical & Fine Arts Museum)

Right — *The Tanaina Indian village of Tyonek sits on the western shore of Cook Inlet, with the massive Alaska Range towering on the horizon. The village was first reported in 1880 as "Toyonok," an Indian name meaning "little chief."* (Steve McCutcheon)

tion of the posts. Not until after United States purchase of Alaska in 1867, when Alaska Commercial Company gained dominance over Alaska trade, did Tyonek regain its former stature as a major trading center.

When miners moved into upper Cook Inlet, first to explore the Hope and Sunrise areas along Turnagain Arm and then to tackle the placers and lodes of the Willow Creek district, Tyonek became a supply and staging area. By the late 1890s, success for commercial fishermen in the area led to construction of a saltery at the mouth of the Chuitna River, two miles north of town.

After the turn of the century, Tyonek's fortunes declined as those of Anchorage prospered. Natural resources, especially game and fish, sustained most of the town's residents, but by mid-century declining stocks of wildlife brought hard times. In 1915, the federal government had established the Tyonek Reservation for Alaska Natives of

that region. When oil was discovered on reservation land decades later, Tyonek residents won the right to prohibit oil development on their land without their permission. With this decision, Tyonek Natives sold oil development rights on their reservation for $12.9 million.

Today community residents have modern homes and facilities and earn their livelihood from wages and subsistence. Not far from their village, Tyonek Timber, Inc., a subsidiary of a Japanese company, leases state land for timber harvest. For the past several years, Tyonek Timber has been logging about 25 million board feet annually, all of which is processed into wood chips and then sent to Japan to be converted into pulp and paper. Land for a camp, chip mill, and dock is leased from Tyonek residents, and the company employs a few Tyonek Natives for its operations.

Perhaps the biggest hope for sustaining Tyonek's economy is exploitation of the Beluga coal fields west of the

Below — *In 1915 the federal government established the Tyonek (also known as Moquawkie) Indian Reservation on the west side of upper Cook Inlet. Years later, Tyonek Natives sold oil development rights on their property, and oil companies set up drill rigs, such as Mobil's Moquawkie wildcat shown here, to search for oil beneath the forested lowlands on the inlet's west side.* (Steve McCutcheon)

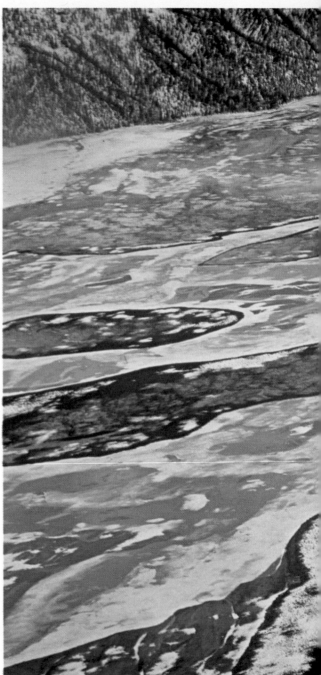

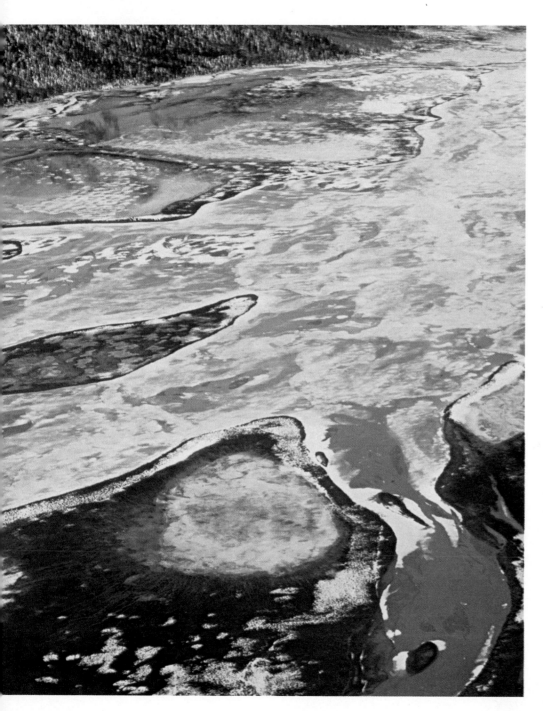

Left — *Late-season ice creates a mosaic in the Neacola River Valley west of Tyonek in the Alaska Range. The Neacola flows into Kenibuna Lake which is separated from larger Chakachamna Lake by a narrow channel pushed against the mountains by Shamrock Glacier.* (John & Margaret Ibbotson)

Above — *Steam rises from the crater of 11,100-foot Mount Spurr, sign of potential pockets of geothermal activity farther down the mountain's flanks. In 1983 state officials may hold their first disposal of land for geothermal development on Spurr's southeastern slopes.* (John & Margaret Ibbotson)

reservation. Alaska officials and foreign investors have explored development of the fields which have the thickest and highest-quality coal beds in the Cook Inlet region. Coal is ranked according to the amount of moisture, sulfur, and other organic matter it contains; the less extraneous material, the higher the quality of coal. In the Beluga field, beds of sub-bituminous coal more than 20 feet thick contribute to the total coal resource in the area of about 1.7 million tons. Private companies are testing the coal and exploring the feasibility of constructing a deepwater port at Tyonek or to the south at Trading Bay for shipment of the coal.

The west side has more than just timber and coal. Chugach Electric Association, Inc., which supplies power to much of Anchorage and indirectly to other portions of the Cook Inlet lowlands, operates a power station at Beluga north of Tyonek. Beluga Station is the largest electricity-generating plant in the state. The facility can produce 326 megawatts of power from eight generating units. Beluga Station, among the largest gas-fired power plants in the nation, sits atop the Beluga River natural gas field. Seven of the plant's eight generating units rely on natural gas for power; the eighth unit operates by waste heat recovery, capturing hot exhaust from two other units.

Geothermal activity also contributes to the overflowing cup of energy-generating potential available on Cook Inlet's west side. In late spring 1983 state officials may hold their first disposal of land for geothermal development. Mount Spurr (11,100 feet), an active volcano about 40 miles northwest of Tyonek, may contain a geothermal treasure chest. Officials will offer 11,000 acres on the mountain's southern flank for geothermal prospecting. The plan calls for prospectors to drill shallow wells to determine water temperature and develop systems for using hot water to generate electricity.

And, of course, there is oil. For the west side this comes primarily in the form of offshore platforms, shore-based

David Fox enjoys a sunny winter day as he snowshoes across High Mountain Lakes in the foothills of the Tordrillo Mountains, part of the Alaska Range. (Shelley Schneider)

Left — *A massive petroleum exploration and production platform stands firmly in Cook Inlet. The first oil well in Alaska was drilled in 1898 at Oil Bay off the Iniskin Peninsula. The well never produced, but further exploration in the inlet led to discoveries of several offshore oil fields. Today there are 13 producing wells in Cook Inlet.* (Steve McCutcheon)

Below — *An ARCO tanker calls at the Drift River loading facility, southwest of Tyonek in Redoubt Bay.*
(John & Margaret Ibbotson, reprinted from *ALASKA GEOGRAPHIC*®)

facilities, and the huge shipping terminal where the Drift River enters Redoubt Bay, 30 miles across Cook Inlet from Kenai. Six oil companies ship oil through Cook Inlet Pipeline Company's line from shore facilities owned by individual companies to the Drift River terminal. From there, the oil is loaded onto tankers for delivery to ports in the Lower 48. In 1981, more than 24.7 million barrels of oil went through the terminal.

The flip side of the resource coin for Cook Inlet's western flank is the abundant fish and game which attract commercial and sport fishermen, hunters, and trappers.

While the Cook Inlet fishery might not be as renowned as that of Bristol Bay or Southeast, the total commercial salmon catch generated $15.5 million for fishermen in 1980. Total value of production from all commercial fisheries taken in the inlet in 1980 reached $109,455,800.

Salmon is the big value catch on the west side where, excluding the take of a drift fleet which fishes both sides of the central inlet, more than half a million salmon were harvested during the 1982 season. The herring fishery is confined to Chinitna and Tuxedni bays where the total catch for 1981 was 134 tons. About 3.28 million pounds of king and tanner crab were taken from the west side in 1981, and 443,144 pounds of razor clams, mostly from Polly Creek and Crescent River, just north of Tuxedni

Bay, were harvested. Most clams taken from the certified beaches must be sold for human consumption; clams harvested from other areas are used as bait in the Dungeness crab fishery on the inlet's east side.

Sport fishermen have not overlooked the more remote regions of the Cook Inlet lowlands either. Lakes and streams on the west side, stretching north as far as the west flank of the Susitna drainage, offer grayling, Dolly Varden, rainbow trout, whitefish, burbot, and all five species of salmon. The Deshka, which enters the Susitna River 36 miles northwest of Anchorage, has one of the state's major king salmon

Left — *Fishermen pick silver salmon from set nets hauled up on the beach near Silver Salmon Creek on Chinitna Bay. More than 600,000 silvers were caught in an August 1982 run up Cook Inlet.* (Gil Mull)

Above — *Ice fishing provides a variety of fresh fish to supplement the winter diets of many Alaska residents. David Fox caught this fresh-water lingcod on a hook and line dropped through a hole in the three feet of ice that covers Judd Lake in winter.* (Shelley Schneider)

Right — *Heinz Allemann crosses a silty glacial stream flowing from Tuxedni Glacier. Many rivers of ice creep down the lofty summits of the Aleutian Range. This glacier extends 16 miles from the slopes of Mount Iliamna to the Tuxedni River.* (Chlaus Lotscher)

Below and right — *The west side of Cook Inlet is an ideal spot for fishermen, hunters, and hikers — many of whom fly to the area from Anchorage. Alexander Lake Lodge, 46 miles north of Tyonek, is one such retreat.*
(Both by Betty Johannsen, reprinted from *ALASKA GEOGRAPHIC®*)

A sport fisherman, trying his hand at catching grayling, watches the approach of a small plane near a stream between Tuxedni and Chinitna bays. (Gil Mull)

Clockwise from left — *"Hey, Mom, look what I caught." David Mull, five, proudly shows off this silver salmon caught in Silver Salmon Creek near Chinitna Bay.* (Gil Mull)

Ester Slwooko cleans cockles at a fish camp near Chinitna Bay during the mid-summer fishing season. Runs of all five species of Pacific salmon draw commercial, sport, and subsistence fishermen to the west side. (Chlaus Lotscher)

Everyone gets into the act during a clamming outing near East Glacier Creek, a 10-mile stream that enters Chinitna Bay 52 miles northwest of Homer. (Gil Mull)

Fishing guide Kevin Kennedy drives a fisherman across Judd Lake nestled in the foothills of the Tordrillo Mountains. The lake is the end of the road for sockeye salmon that run up the Talachulitna River on their way to spawning beds at the west end of the lake. (Shelley Schneider)

fisheries. Anglers pull trophy rainbows from the Talachulitna, which meets the Skwentna River northwest of Tyonek, and then flows into the Yentna River before dumping into Cook Inlet.

For hunters, the west side, particularly in the north, offers bountiful game. Moose thrive in willows in the lowlands. The majority of Dall sheep in the area inhabit western slopes of the Aleutian and Alaska ranges, but a few do cross over, especially near mountain passes. But there is one obstacle to hunting on the west side: access is difficult because there are few places to land a small plane. Inlet beaches, gravel bars, and a few lakes provide the only suitable landing sites. Some hunters search for prey from boats.

Moving from the north to the south along the west side, the habitat changes from forests and brush to open tundra. The wildlife changes also. Where black bears are common in

Hunting and fishing take on an added challenge on the west side where few suitable landing sites are available for small planes bringing outdoor enthusiasts from Anchorage and the Kenai Peninsula. The pilot of this Cessna 185 finds a sandy beach at Chakachamna Lake to his liking. Among the largest lakes of the region, Chakachamna extends 15 miles between the Tordrillo and Chigmit mountains. (Nancy Tankersley)

forests to the north, their larger cousins, brown bears, take over in the open country to the south.

Speaking of brown bears, there is no better place to view them than at McNeil River State Game Sanctuary on Kamishak Bay, across the inlet from the tip of the Kenai Peninsula. Here the salmon, in particular the large chum runs, draw as many as 30 brown bears per day to fish at a falls about one and a half miles up the McNeil River.

Dave Bean (left) and Tom Brennan restrain their retrievers from chasing the air taxi as it leaves on the 20-minute flight to Anchorage. Located near Mount Susitna and just west of the Susitna River, the duck shack rests on short stilts to keep the building out of the water during occasional 32-foot tides which cover the entire Susitna Flats. These hunters, with hundreds of others in the Anchorage area, traditionally observe the September 1 opening day of duck season with a pilgrimage to "the flats." Mallards, wigeons, pintails, shovelers, and other ducks, as well as Canada geese are found on shallow lakes and ponds of the flats. (Tom Gresham, staff)

Left — *A semipermanent Alaska hunting camp, complete with wood stove, nestles among the trees on the west side.* (Leland Brun, reprinted from *ALASKA GEOGRAPHIC®*)

Below — *Spruce grouse, common in coniferous and mixed forests of Cook Inlet country, add variety to the stew pot of west side residents. This grouse was photographed sunning itself in late spring on a game trail.* (Shelley Schneider)

Left — *Here is what hunters on the west side hope to bring home — a bull moose, largest member of North America's deer family. Moose eat a variety of vegetation, but prefer willow, birch, and aspen.* (Martin Grosnick)

Right — *One of the most elegant furbearers of Cook Inlet country, red foxes are highly prized by trappers seeking the mammal's golden, silky fur.* (Norma Dudiak)

Floatplanes, usually from Homer, ferry visitors across the inlet to a camp on a small spit reaching into McNeil Cove. Visitors, whose names have been selected in a drawing for a four-day permit, must bring tents, food, and all their gear. Biologists from the Alaska Department of Fish & Game manage the sanctuary and limit the number of visitors to 10 per day for the six weeks the bears are at the falls.

McNeil offers more than just bears. Occasionally a red fox will come by to check out the commotion at the river. Harbor seals follow the salmon into the cove. Eagles and gulls serve as clean-up crews, picking up bits of fish left by the bears.

Brown bears are the number one target for sport hunters coming to the lower inlet's west side. But the few year-round residents concentrate on moose, not nearly as abundant as they are farther north. Trappers set their snares for beaver, river otter, coyote, and fox. A few pockets of muskrats and some mink add to the trappers' take.

Left — *A little rain, or even a lot of rain, doesn't stop this Beaver from Kachemak Air Service from taking off at McNeil River. Most visitors to McNeil are flown across the inlet from Homer or Kenai.* (Don Cornelius)

Above — *It's time to take five for some of the photographers that gather at McNeil River to photograph the concentrations of brown bears. Visitors are limited to 10 per day; names are chosen in a drawing by Alaska Department of Fish & Game personnel.* (Don Cornelius)

Right — *Mom and her two cubs check out the fare at McNeil River State Game Sanctuary, a chief wildlife viewing site on the west side. Brown bears congregate at the river during the salmon runs of July and August.* (Third Eye Photography)

Above — *Lake Clark Pass, 1,000 feet, is 50 miles west-northwest of Kenai and provides access to its namesake from Cook Inlet.* (Bureau of Land Management, reprinted from *ALASKA GEOGRAPHIC®*)

Below — *Many Alaskans, particularly bush residents, heat their homes with wood throughout the winter. This rural Alaskan unloads spruce logs from a boat onto the dock at Judd Lake. Because he cut his wood in October before the lake froze over, a boat provided an efficient means of transporting the heavy logs across the lake to his cabin.* (Shelley Schneider)

Left — *Photographer Chlaus Lotscher describes his close encounter with the flying kind: "My climbing partner and I were a few hundred feet below the summit of Mount Iliamna when a fish-transporting plane flew by and discovered us. They took a closer look by circling high above us, then circled again, this time closer. They disappeared in clouds, and we thought they had gone. Not so. After a few minutes, the plane came out deep under us, flying towards the west wall of Iliamna which we had just climbed. They were flying toward us and finally winged by at almost the same level we were standing. We saw a hand waving out the window."*

Below — *A fumarole spouts atop the 10,016-foot summit of Mount Iliamna. When cloud cover obscures either Iliamna or its neighbor to the north, Redoubt, the two mountains can be confused. Iliamna can be identified by three peaks on its left side when viewed from the east.* (George Ripley)

Left — Two of the volcanic peaks crowning the Aleutian Range are (foreground) Mount Redoubt (10,197 feet) and Mount Iliamna (10,016 feet). Mount Redoubt's most recent eruption of any consequence occurred in 1966. The mountain gave off mostly steam at that time, but the heat was great enough to melt much of the glacier on the northern flank which brought about flooding along the Drift River. Mount Redoubt's activities are closely monitored by oil company executives because of the shipping terminal for oil at the river's mouth.
(John & Margaret Ibbotson)

Above — *Sea otters can be found in the shallow coastal waters of lower Cook Inlet, where they feed on shellfish and other marine invertebrates. Sea otter fur, considered to be the finest fur in the world, was sought by some of the earliest explorers of the inlet.*
(Norma Dudiak)

Left — *Aleut men paddle a three-hatch* bidarka *on Iniskin Bay across the inlet from Homer. Russian fur traders brought Aleuts to lower Cook Inlet to hunt the prized furbearers. The three-hatch* bidarka *was developed in the far western Aleutian Islands and brought eastward by the Russians sometime after 1750.* (Anchorage Historical & Fine Arts Museum)

Cormorants (foreground), murres, and a few gulls perch on this rocky outcropping in Cook Inlet. Numerous seabird species feed on the abundant marine life of the inlet's west side.
(Norma Dudiak)

A mature bull walrus suns himself on a rock at the northwest corner of Kalgin Island in summer 1982. According to the photographer, the animal has returned to the same spot for three of the last four summers; no other walrus have been observed in the area. Pacific walrus are normally found in the Bering and Chukchi seas.
(John Crandall)

Four major islands break the surface of Cook Inlet: Fire Island off Anchorage; and three islands guarding bays along the west side. Set netters and moose hunters make their way to 13-mile-long Kalgin Island off Redoubt Bay.

A few fishermen and a multitude of seabirds call Chisik Island, off Tuxedni Bay and part of Alaska Maritime National Wildlife Refuge, their summer home. Thousands of black-legged kittiwakes, common murres, tufted and horned puffins, glaucous-winged gulls, and a scattering of cormorants, bald eagles, and peregrine falcons find the island to their liking. On the mainland opposite Chisik, Lake Clark National Park and Preserve touches Cook Inlet. Set aside by the Alaska National Interest Lands Conservation Act, Lake Clark preserves about 3.6 million acres of mountain and coastal wonderland, a melange of glaciers, snow-capped peaks, volcanoes, forested valleys, tundra, and untouched beaches.

To the south, taking in part of the shoreline of Kamishak Bay and encompassing more than four million acres, lies Katmai National Park and Preserve, an expansion of the older Katmai National Monument. Designated by the same legislation that established Lake Clark park and preserve, Katmai promotes the volcanic landscape of the Valley of Ten Thousand Smokes and the twisted, indented coastline of the lower inlet's west side.

Gatepost to Kamishak Bay is Augustine Island with its fiery volcano that dusted the Cook Inlet lowlands with ash in 1976. Most active of the inlet's volcanoes, Augustine spit out billowing clouds of steam and sent ash rising to more than 40,000 feet. Avalanches of gas and pumice sped down the mountain at speeds of from 60 to 160 miles an hour.

Augustine is at once the beginning and the end of this tour of Cook Inlet country. As the explosive mountain spewed forth steam, ash, and pumice, it altered the landscape, bringing forth new soil and blasting away the mountaintop. So it goes in the Cook Inlet basin . . . constant change, constant growth. Sixty-eight years ago Anchorage did not exist. Today the city embraces the largest metropolitan area within a thousand miles and more than half the state's population. Anchorage triggers the commercial pulse, but the country is still there. And the wilderness, an integral part of the Alaska mystique, still calls.

Above — *Kevin Crandall gets ready to grab the buoy and pick up a set net at the end of a fishing period on Kalgin Island. Each period lasts 12 hours, and there are normally two periods a week throughout the summer season. The total 1982 catch from the island's 15 to 20 set net sites was 117,407 salmon, mostly sockeye and coho. (John Greely)*

Right — *Crew members from a fishing tender pick up a load of salmon off the north end of Kalgin Island. (Tom Walker)*

Left — *Black-legged kittiwakes and cormorants share a rocky cliff on Chisik Island, at the mouth of Tuxedni Bay.* (Nancy Simmerman, reprinted from *ALASKA GEOGRAPHIC*®)

Above — *Blue water and rocky cliffs mark the entrance to Tuxedni Bay, on the west side of Cook Inlet. The Chigmit Mountains rise in the background.* (Gil Mull)

Below — *Peaks south of Tuxedni Bay and north of Mount Iliamna create a spectacular vista for this hiker about to cross the wetlands of Tuxedni Bay.* (Chlaus Lotscher)

Above — *At low tide, these two fishing boats ride high and dry on a mud bar tucked into a narrow stretch of Iliamna Bay, an arm of Kamishak Bay. Chum salmon, and lesser runs of pink and coho salmon, lure fishermen to the Kamishak area.* (Raymond J. Frank)

Right — *Cutting 5,730 feet into the atmosphere, knife-edged ridges of The Tusks guide pilots through Merrill Pass in the Alaska Range.* (John & Margaret Ibbotson)

Alaska Geographic® Back Issues

The North Slope, Vol. 1, No. 1. The charter issue of *ALASKA GEOGRAPHIC*® took a long, hard look at the North Slope and the then-new petroleum development at "the top of the world." *Out of print.*

One Man's Wilderness, Vol. 1, No. 2. The story of a dream shared by many, fulfilled by few: a man goes into the bush, builds a cabin and shares his incredible wilderness experience. Color photos. 116 pages, $9.95

Admiralty . . . Island in Contention, Vol. 1, No. 3. An intimate and multifaceted view of Admiralty: its geological and historical past, its present-day geography, wildlife and sparse human population. Color photos. 78 pages, $5.00

Fisheries of the North Pacific: History, Species, Gear & Processes, Vol. 1, No. 4. The title says it all. This volume is out of print, but the book, from which it was excerpted, is available in a revised, expanded large-format volume. 424 pages. $24.95.

The Alaska-Yukon Wild Flowers Guide, Vol. 2, No. 1. First Northland flower book with both large, color photos and detailed drawings of every species described. Features 160 species, common and scientific names and growing height. Vertical-format book edition now available. 218 pages, $12.95.

Richard Harrington's Yukon, Vol. 2, No. 2. The Canadian province with the colorful past *and* present. *Out of print.*

Prince William Sound, Vol. 2, No. 3. This volume explored the people and resources of the Sound. *Out of print.*

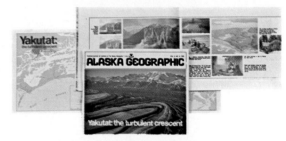

Yakutat: The Turbulent Crescent, Vol. 2, No. 4. History, geography, people — and the impact of the coming of the oil industry. *Out of print.*

Glacier Bay: Old Ice, New Land, Vol. 3, No. 1. The expansive wilderness of Southeastern Alaska's Glacier Bay National Monument (recently proclaimed a national park and preserve) unfolds in crisp text and color photographs. Records the flora and fauna of the area, its natural history, with hike and cruise information, plus a large-scale color map. 132 pages, $9.95

The Land: Eye of the Storm, Vol. 3, No. 2. The future of one of the earth's biggest pieces of real estate! *This volume is out of print,* but the latest on the Alaska lands controversy is detailed completely in Volume 8, Number 4.

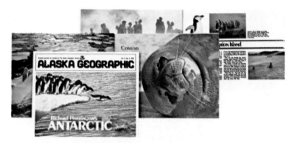

Richard Harrington's Antarctic, Vol. 3, No. 3. The Canadian photojournalist guides readers through remote and little understood regions of the Antarctic and Subantarctic. More than 200 color photos and a large fold-out map. 104 pages, $8.95

The Silver Years of the Alaska Canned Salmon Industry: An Album of Historical Photos, Vol. 3, No. 4. The grand and glorious past of the Alaska canned salmon industry. *Out of print.*

Alaska's Volcanoes: Northern Link in the Ring of Fire, Vol. 4, No. 1. Scientific overview supplemented with eyewitness accounts of Alaska's historic volcano eruptions. Includes color and black-and-white photos and a schematic description of the effects of plate movement upon volcanic activity. 88 pages. *Temporarily out of print.*

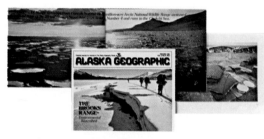

The Brooks Range: Environmental Watershed, Vol. 4, No. 2. An impressive work on a truly impressive piece of Alaska — The Brooks Range. *Out of print.*

Kodiak: Island of Change, Vol. 4, No. 3. Russians, wildlife, logging and even petroleum . . . an island where change is one of the few constants. *Out of print.*

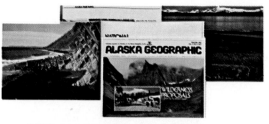

Wilderness Proposals: Which Way for Alaska's Lands?, Vol. 4, No. 4. This volume gave yet another detailed analysis of the many Alaska lands questions. *Out of print.*

Cook Inlet Country, Vol. 5, No. 1. Our first comprehensive look at the area. A visual tour of the region — its communities, big and small, and its countryside. Begins at the southern tip of the Kenai Peninsula, circles Turnagain Arm and Knik Arm for a close-up view of Anchorage, and visits the Matanuska and Susitna valleys and the wild, west side of the inlet. *Out of print.*

Southeast: Alaska's Panhandle, Vol. 5, No. 2. Explores Southeastern Alaska's maze of fjords and islands, mossy forests and glacier-draped mountains — from Dixon Entrance to Icy Bay, including all of the state's fabled Inside Passage. Along the way are profiles of every town, together with a look at the region's history, economy, people, attractions and future. Includes large fold-out map and seven area maps. 192 pages, $12.95.

Bristol Bay Basin, Vol. 5, No. 3. Explores the land and the people of the region known to many as the commercial salmon-fishing capital of Alaska. Illustrated with contemporary color and historic black-and-white photos. Includes a large fold-out map of the region. *Out of print.*

Alaska Whales and Whaling, Vol. 5, No. 4. The wonders of whales in Alaska — their life cycles, travels and travails — are examined, with an authoritative history of commercial and subsistence whaling in the North. Includes a fold-out poster of 14 major whale species in Alaska in perspective, color photos and illustrations, with historical photos and line drawings. 144 pages, $12.95.

Yukon-Kuskokwim Delta, Vol. 6, No. 1. This volume explored the people and lifestyles of one of the most remote areas of the 49th state. *Out of print.*

The Aurora Borealis, Vol. 6, No. 2. Here one of the world's leading experts — Dr. S.-I. Akasofu of the University of Alaska — explains in an easily understood manner, aided by many diagrams and spectacular color and black-and-white photos, what causes the aurora, how it works, how and why scientists are studying it today and its implications for our future. 96 pages, $7.95.

Alaska's Native People, Vol. 6, No. 3. In this edition the editors examine the varied worlds of the Inupiat Eskimo, Yup'ik Eskimo, Athabascan, Aleut, Tlingit, Haida and Tsimshian. Included are sensitive, informative articles by Native writers, plus a large, four-color map detailing the Native villages and defining the language areas. 304 pages, $24.95.

The Stikine, Vol. 6, No 4. River route to three Canadian gold strikes in the 1800s. This edition explores 400 miles of Stikine wilderness, recounts the river's paddlewheel past and looks into the future. Illustrated with contemporary color photos and historic black-and-white; includes a large fold-out map. 96 pages, $9.95.

Alaska's Great Interior, Vol. 7, No. 1. Alaska's rich Interior country, west from the Alaska-Yukon Territory border and including the huge drainage between the Alaska Range and the Brooks Range, is covered thoroughly. Included are the region's people, communities, history, economy, wilderness areas and wildlife. Illustrated with contemporary color and black-and-white photos. Includes a large fold-out map. 128 pages, $9.95.

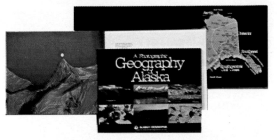

A Photographic Geography of Alaska, Vol. 7, No. 2. An overview of the entire state — a visual tour through the six regions of Alaska: Southeast, Southcentral/Gulf Coast, Alaska Peninsula and Aleutians, Bering Sea Coast, Arctic and Interior. Plus a handy appendix of valuable information — "Facts About Alaska." Approximately 160 color and black-and-white photos and 35 maps. 192 pages, $14.95.

The Aleutians, Vol. 7, No. 3. Home of the Aleut, a tremendous wildlife spectacle, a major World War II battleground and now the heart of a thriving new commercial fishing industry. Contemporary color and black-and-white photographs, and a large fold-out map. 224 pages, $14.95.

Klondike Lost: A Decade of Photographs by Kinsey & Kinsey, Vol. 7, No. 4. An album of rare photographs and all-new text about the lost Klondike boom town of Grand Forks, second in size only to Dawson during the gold rush. Introduction by noted historian Pierre Berton: 138 pages, area maps and more than 100 historical photos, most never before published. $12.95.

Wrangell-Saint Elias, Vol. 8, No. 1. Mountains, including the continent's second- and fourth-highest peaks, dominate this international wilderness that sweeps from the Wrangell Mountains in Alaska to the southern Saint Elias range in Canada. Illustrated with contemporary color and historical black-and-white photographs. Includes a large fold-out map. 144 pages, $9.95.

Alaska Mammals, Vol. 8, No. 2. From tiny ground squirrels to the powerful polar bear, and from the tundra hare to the magnificent whales inhabiting Alaska's waters, this volume includes 80 species of mammals found in Alaska. Included are beautiful color photographs and personal accounts of wildlife encounters. 184 pages, $12.95.

The Kotzebue Basin, Vol. 8, No. 3. Examines northwestern Alaska's thriving trading area of Kotzebue Sound and the Kobuk and Noatak river basins. Contemporary color and historical black-and-white photographs. 184 pages, $12.95.

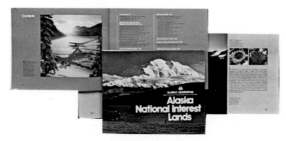

Alaska National Interest Lands, Vol. 8, No. 4. Following passage of the bill formalizing Alaska's national interest land selections (d-2 lands), longtime Alaskans Celia Hunter and Ginny Wood review each selection, outlining location, size, access, and briefly describing the region's special attractions. Illustrated with contemporary color photographs. 242 pages, $14.95.

Alaska's Glaciers, Vol. 9, No. 1. Examines in-depth the massive rivers of ice, their composition, exploration, present-day distribution and scientific significance. Illustrated with many contemporary color and historical-black-and-white photos, the text includes separate discussions of more than a dozen glacial regions. 144 pages, $9.95.

Sitka and Its Ocean/Island World, Vol. 9, No. 2. From the elegant capital of Russian America to a beautiful but modern port, Sitka, on Baranof Island, has become a commercial and cultural center for Southeastern Alaska. Pat Roppel, longtime Southeast resident and expert on the region's history, examines in detail the past and present of Sitka, Baranof Island, and neighboring Chichagof Island. Illustrated with contemporary color and historical black-and-white photographs. 128 pages, $9.95.

Islands of the Seals: The Pribilofs, Vol. 9, No. 3.
Great herds of northern fur seals drew Russians and Aleuts to these remote Bering Sea islands where they founded permanent communities and established a unique international commerce. The communities languished under U.S. control until recent decades when new legislation and attempts at economic diversification have increased interest in the islands, their Aleut people, and the rich marine resources nearby. Illustrated with contemporary color and historical black-and-white photographs. 128 pages, $9.95.

Alaska's Oil/Gas & Minerals Industry, Vol. 9, No. 4. Experts detail the geological processes and resulting mineral and fossil fuel resources that are now in the forefront of Alaska's economy. Discussions of historical methods and the latest techniques in present-day mining, submarine deposits, taxes, regulations, and education complete this overview of an important state industry. Illustrated with historical black-and-white and contemporary color photographs. 216 pages, $12.95.

Adventure Roads North: The Story of the Alaska Highway and Other Roads in *The MILEPOST*®, Vol. 10, No. 1. From Alaska's first highway — the Richardson — to the famous Alaska Highway, first overland route to the 49th state, text and photos provide a history of Alaska's roads and take a mile-by-mile look at the country they cross. 224 pages, $14.95.

NEXT ISSUE
Alaska's Salmon Fisheries, Vol. 10, No. 3.
The work of *ALASKA*® magazine Outdoors Editor Jim Rearden, this issue takes a comprehensive look at Alaska's most valuable commercial fishery. Through text and photos, readers will learn about the five species of salmon caught in Alaska, different types of fishing gear and how each works, and will take a district-by-district tour of salmon fisheries throughout the state. To members in August 1983. Price to be announced.

The Alaska Geographic Society

Box 4-EEE, Anchorage, AK 99509

Membership in The Alaska Geographic Society is $30, which includes the following year's four quarterlies which explore a wide variety of subjects in the Northland, each issue an adventure in great photos, maps, and excellent research. Members receive their quarterlies as part of the membership fee at considerable savings over the prices which nonmembers must pay for individual book editions.

Unfolded copies of the two illustrated Cook Inlet maps that are included in this issue are available. To order the set of two maps (Cook Inlet "today" and Cook Inlet "future") send your name, address, and $7.95 plus $1.00 for postage and handling (U.S. funds) to: The Alaska Geographic Society, Box 4-EEE, Anchorage, Alaska 99509.